W9-AQT-662

TWAYNE'S WORLD AUTHORS SERIES

A Survey of the World's Literature

Sylvia E. Bowman, Indiana University

GENERAL EDITOR

FRANCE

Maxwell A. Smith, Guerry Professor of French, Emeritus
The University of Chattanooga
Former Visiting Professor in Modern Languages
The Florida State University

EDITOR

Théophile Gautier

TWAS 362

Théophile Gautier

Théophile Gautier

By RICHARD B. GRANT
University of Texas at Austin

TWAYNE PUBLISHERS
A DIVISION OF G. K. HALL & CO., BOSTON

Library of Congress Cataloging in Publication Data

Grant, Richard B.
Théophile Gautier.

(Twayne's world authors series; TWAS 362: France)
Includes bibliography and index.
1. Gautier, Théophile, 1811 - 1872.
PQ2258.Z5G7 848'.7'09 [B] 75-4819
ISBN 0-8057-6213-2

MANUFACTURED IN THE UNITED STATES OF AMERICA

To Carolyn,
who gave so much

Contents

About the Author

Richard B. Grant earned his B.A. and his Ph.D. degrees at Harvard, and taught French language and literature for many years at Duke University. In 1971 he joined the faculty of the University of Texas at Austin as a Professor of French. In addition to collaborating in the writing of two textbooks, he is the author of *Zola's* Son Excellence Eugène Rougon: *An Historical and Critical Study, The Perilous Quest: Image, Myth, and Prophecy in the Narratives of Victor Hugo,* and *The Goncourt Brothers* (Twayne, 1972). He has also written many articles on nineteenth-century French fiction.

Preface

Théophile Gautier was primarily a poet and writer of fiction, but he made many other contributions to the history of nineteenth-century French literature as well. He joined the young Romantics of 1830 in their struggle to overthrow the neoclassical establishment and was later a champion of the doctrine of Art for Art's sake. He also wrote plays and ballet librettos and was creative in the field of travel literature. Finally, he was for many years an influential critic of literature and art for the Parisian press.

A short book covering Gautier's creativity requires one to choose between a superficial overview and a detailed examination of a few texts. Since in the case of Gautier neither of these approaches is fully satisfactory, I have tried to combine the two in an effort to give a broad picture of his work and yet at the same time to treat a few texts in detail. But anyone conversant with the extent of Gautier's writing will realize — as does the present writer — how much more could have been included. Only minor writers can be thoroughly treated in two hundred pages.

A word concerning translation is in order. I have given prose quotations only in English. As for the poetry, I have given it in the original French with a straightforward prose translation immediately following in the case of short quotations and in the notes at the end of the book in the case of more lengthy passages. In all cases the translations are my own.

Finally, I would like to express my appreciation to the University Research Institute of the University of Texas at Austin for a summer travel grant to Paris to consult certain periodicals.

RICHARD B. GRANT

University of Texas at Austin

Chronology

Unless otherwise indicated, all publication dates below are for the years in which the work appeared in volume form. Frequently there was an earlier newspaper publication.

1811 August 30, birth of Pierre-Jules-Théophile Gautier in Tarbes to Pierre and Adelaïde Gautier.

1814 Family moves to Paris.

1817 January 11, birth of a sister, Emilie.

1820 March 12, birth of a sister, Zoé.

1822 January 9, Gautier enters Collège Louis-le-Grand as boarding student. April 23, leaves for reasons of health. October, enters the Collège Charlemagne as day student.

1829 Studies painting at the Rioult studio. June 27, meets Victor Hugo.

1830 February 25, battle of *Hernani.* Victor Hugo moves next door to the Gautiers, now residing at no. 8 Place des Vosges. July 28, publication of Gautier's first volume of poetry, *Poésies.*

1831 First article published in *Le Mercure de France au XIXe siècle.*

1832 Becomes a member of the *petit cénacle.* Publication of *Albertus, ou l'âme et le péché.*

1833 Publication of *Les Jeunes-France, romans goguenards.*

1834 Family moves to Passy. Gautier remains behind in the Impasse du Doyenné.

1834 - 1835 Publication of some of the articles which will form *Les Grotesques.*

1835 - 1836 Publication of *Mademoiselle de Maupin.*

1836 February, beginning of his liaison with Eugénie Fort. July - August, trip with Gérard de Nerval to Belgium and Holland. November 29, birth of a son, Théophile Gautier. Begins career as critic for *La Presse*. Publication of "Fortunio" under the title "El Dorado."

1838 Publication of *La Comédie de la mort*.

1839 Publication of *Une Larme du diable*.

1840 May 5, leaves for Spain with Eugène Piot; returns October 7.

1841 June 28, premiere of the ballet, *Giselle*, danced by Carlotta Grisi.

1843 Publication of *Voyage en Espagne* under the title *Tra los montes*. Premiere of ballet, *La Péri*, danced by Carlotta Grisi.

1844 Ernesta Grisi becomes Gautier's mistress. Publication in volume form of *Les Grotesques*.

1845 First performance of comedy, *Le Tricorne enchanté*. Voyage to Algeria. Edition of *Poésies complètes* published. August 25, birth of a daughter, Judith, to Gautier and Ernesta Grisi.

1847 First performance of comedy, *Pierrot posthume*. November 28, birth of a daughter, Estelle.

1848 July 7, death of mother.

1849 Beginning of liaison with Marie Mattéi.

1850 July 31, leaves for Italy; returns November 4.

1851 January 15, premiere of ballet, *Pâquerette*.

1852 Publication of *Un Trio de romans* (including "Arria Marcella"), *Caprices et zigzags*, *Emaux et camées*, *Italia (Voyage en Italie)*. August 28, leaves Paris for Constantinople, Athens, and Venice; returns in October. End of liaison with Marie Mattéi.

1853 Publication of *Constantinople*.

1854 May 31, premiere of ballet, *Gemma*. August 22, death of Gautier's father.

1855 Publication of *Les Beaux-Arts en Europe*. Leaves *La Presse* to work for *Le Moniteur universel*.

1856 First unsuccessful attempt to be elected to the Académie Française. Publication of *L'Art moderne*.

1857 Publication of "Avatar" and "Jettatura."

1858 Publication of *Le Roman de la momie*. April 22, premiere of ballet, *Yanko le bandit*. July 14, premiere of ballet, *Sacountala*. Gautier named Officer of the Legion of Honor. September 15, leaves for Russia. Publication of *Honoré de Balzac*.

1858 - 1859 Publication of *Histoire de l'art dramatique en France depuis vingt-cinq ans.*

1859 March 27, returns to Paris from Russia.

1861 Publication of *Trésors d'art de la Russie ancienne et moderne.*

1863 Publication of *Le Capitaine Fracasse* and *Romans et contes.*

1864 - 1866 Frequent trips to Geneva to visit Carlotta Grisi.

1865 Publication of *Loin de Paris.*

1866 Publication of "Spirite."

1867 Publication of *Voyage en Russie.*

1869 Trip to Egypt for inauguration of Suez canal.

1871 Publication of *Tableaux de siège.*

1872 Definitive edition of *Emaux et camées.* Publication of *Théâtre* and *Histoire du romantisme* begins appearing in the newspaper. October 23, death of Gautier from heart condition.

CHAPTER 1

The Formative Years

I *Childhood and Adolescence*

THERE have been many legends associated with the birth of Théophile Gautier, including one that he was conceived in the dilapidated castle of d'Artagnan. Modern scholars have discredited these fanciful tales, which were merely well-meaning efforts after the fact to try to invest Gautier with an origin in harmony with his innate aristocratic temperament. The facts of the matter are much less dramatic. In 1810 Pierre Gautier, a minor government official, married one Antoinette-Adelaïde Cocarde. A son, Pierre-Jules-Théophile was born to them on August 30, 1811, in the city of Tarbes in southwestern France. In 1814 Pierre was transferred to Paris where the family took up residence in the rue du Temple. Théophile was destined to be a Parisian.

What little we know of Gautier's youth comes to us largely from the poet himself. Years later he recalled fondly certain episodes of his early childhood in a brief autobiographical sketch.[1] If the factual details given in this account are often unverifiable and are even occasionally inaccurate, his recollections at least give an accurate picture of how he felt about those early years. Every critic has noted that the poet had an intense feeling of nostalgia for his childhood, and in a perceptive study, H. Van der Tuin suggests that Gautier never quite resolved his infantile attachment to his mother with the result that he forever longed to return to the distant paradise of the womb and was condemned to an endless search for an idealized female figure. This unresolved problem, Van der Tuin goes on to deduce, left Gautier with a split in his personality, making it difficult for him to reconcile the reality of life with his dreams of perfection.[2] Psychological interpretations of writers long dead are risky at best, but all critics agree that Gautier had a deep-seated longing for an idealized world. Perhaps Van der Tuin is correct in his explanation, for Gautier's description of the city of his birth tends to support the idea of a maternal fixation. Gautier claimed that more than forty years later he could still recall the house in which he was born and "the outline of the blue mountains silhouetted against the horizon and the many streams that flowed through town."[3] A Freudian critic has little trouble in seeing in the protective walls of the home and the surrounding mountains with the flowing water more than topographical reality. There is in Gautier's shaping of his earliest recollections a strong suggestion of the maternal womb. But even if one stops short of a Freudian interpretation, home and mountains point to Gautier's need for an ideal place of security, and the streams indicate that this landscape, as a place of living waters, is a genuine paradise. Already we see Gautier eager to find a refuge from the cares and frustrations of the real world. This longing for a distant paradise was expressed in other ways as well. In the same self-portrait, for instance, Gautier described himself when a boy as resembling "a young Spanish Cuban, sensitive to the cold and nostalgic for his homeland,"[4] as if he were already an exile from an island paradise. Biographers have had a tendency to take this description at face value, for Gautier was dark of complexion. But a glance at his photographs really suggests no necessity for such a comparison. In fact, Gautier gave himself many ancestries. He would often refer to his long "Merovingian" hair; he was also to dress on occasion in Arab garb, and in matters sexual, he considered himself something of a Turk. In short, whether Cuban, or Turkish or or African, Gautier was being less descriptive than metaphoric. For the Western imagination, a tropical paradise offers the natural bounty of the earth, which makes work unnecessary; it offers beautiful, ardent women who gladly renew a man's youth; above all, it abolishes the cold seasons. Fall and winter disappear, and with their disappearance, time is abolished, and there is no more death. Paul Gauguin would later in the century try to turn this dream into a reality.

Gautier's early reading reflected this tendency in him. His two favorite childhood books dazzled his youthful imagination with the wonders of idyllic island paradises. One was Defoe's *Robinson Crusoe*. "I couldn't think of anything," he wrote, "except desert islands and living free in the bosom of nature, and I would build under the living-room table cabins out of logs where I would hide out for hours on end."[5] The other book was Bernardin de Saint-Pierre's *Paul et Virginie* (1787), a best seller in its time. The romance describes the lush island paradise of Madagascar as the idealized setting for an equally idealized action. Gautier claimed later that not even Shakespeare, Byron, or Hugo ever put him in such a state of intoxication as did *Paul et Virginie*.

Finally, it is appropriate to point out the importance of his childhood hobbies. One was building model ships (correctly rigged, he claimed), as if he were concretizing a wish to sail off to a distant and better land. Another, to which he returned in his later years, was a passion for building marionette theaters. He constructed his own stage and painted his own décor, as if creating a tiny, artificial universe of his own that he could control.

Schooling has a way of interrupting boyish daydreams, however. On January 9, 1822, he was placed as a boarding student *(interne)* in the Collège Louis-le-Grand. His life had been most pleasant at home. His father was indulgent, and he enjoyed the company of his two sisters, Lili and Zoé. He found boarding school a shock: "I was seized by a total despair that nothing could conquer. The brutality and noisiness of my little prison mates horrified me. I was dying of cold, boredom and isolation within those tall, sad walls."[6] The food was bad and at least one teacher hostile. His health began to deteriorate, and after three months, on April 23, he was brought home. He finished his schooling as a day pupil at the Collège Charlemagne. So precious was his freedom that on each of his homework papers, after his name, he would put the words *externe libre* (free day student). Happier now, hardworking, and aided by his father, who took a keen interest in his education, Gautier finished his studies in a very creditable manner.

During the summer, while still in school, Théophile would accompany his parents to the village of Mauperthuis, southeast of Paris. In the preface to the first volume of his poetry, he evoked the charm of the locale. "There are modest landscapes, in the Flemish manner . . . no great mountains or endless vistas; no torrents or cataracts. Gentle plains with a cobalt blue backdrop, humble lined hillsides, with a road winding through them; a thatched hut with smoke rising, a stream gurgling under the water lilies." And if we may make the somewhat risky assumption that the rural landscape described by the hero of *Mademoiselle de Maupin*, Albert, is a direct transposition of the countryside at Mauperthuis, we may add the following idyllic vision: "How suited we were to be part of the landscape! — How well we went with the gentle repose of nature here, how easily we harmonized with it! Springtime without, youth within, sun on the lawn, a smile on our lips, snowy flowers on each bush, white illusions within our souls, modest blushes on our cheeks and on the wild roses. . . . What evenings we spent there walking slowly, so near the water that often we had one foot in it and the other out."[7] Other possible details taken from *Mademoiselle de Maupin* were an avenue bordered with trees, a crossroads with an obelisk of sorts, a church steeple. It takes no great sagacity, however, to note that the descriptions are highly conventionalized. There is nothing here that could not apply reasonably well to any other quiet village landscape, real or literary, and any topographical evidence intended to prove the accuracy of the description is bound to be as illusory as the search for the village, say, in which the action of Flaubert's *Madame Bovary* was supposed to have taken place. It is an idealized scene which owes at least as much to the pastoral tradition as it does to the realities of Mauperthuis. Gautier's insistence on how well he and his playmates were in harmony with nature makes clear that the landscape serves the function of psychic projection: the peace and unity of the countryside reflect an inner calm that in later years he felt he could rarely recapture. By the magic of selective memory, Gautier was creating yet another of his evanescent terrestrial paradises.

At this point, he began to move in the direction of his life's commitment. Already in school he had gone beyond the routine assignments and treated the subjects of Latin poetry in every imaginable meter, and his taste tended to be as exotic as some of his daydreams: "I enjoyed imitating styles that they called 'decadent' at school. I was often accused of barbarism and Africanism, and I was delighted, as if it were a compliment."[8] But literature was not his only form of experimentation. As would his friends Jules and Edmond de Goncourt a generation later, he also tried his hand at painting. He had been sketching (as well as painting puppet theater décor) since the age of seven. Fortunately for young Théo, his middle-class family was not at all opposed to an artistic career. The family friend and mentor, Father Montesquiou, urged Pierre Gautier to have the boy take painting lessons. And so in the spring of 1829, while still a student at the Collège Charlemagne, he began to attend the studio of the painter Rioult. From a strictly artistic point of view, the experience did not work out well. Gautier had facility but no technique and was either unwilling or unable to start over again from the beginning. His nearsightedness may have hindered him as well. But if Gautier was not destined to succeed as a painter, the months spent in the studio were of great importance, paradoxically, to his entry into the world of literature.

At eighteen, Théophile was no longer delicate of body. He had learned to love swimming and other forms of physical exercise. Workouts at the Petit swimming pool had developed a physique of which he was positively vain. Now his social maturation could keep pace with the physical. Having lived at home in a protected family circle, he needed to be out among other people. In the artist's studio he enjoyed the noisy camaraderie and, more significantly, heard others talk about the new Romanticism and its desire to transcend the limitations of this world in a search for the absolute. This attitude could not fail to appeal to a dreamer of paradises lost. And so increasingly, especially as he realized that he would never succeed as a painter, Gautier moved into the world of letters. It was not long before he was an enthusiastic admirer of the works of Chateaubriand, Byron, and Scott. At the Collège Charlemagne, Gautier had already become a close friend of Gérard de Nerval, the translator (in 1827) of Goethe's *Faust*. Through Nerval, Gautier met Pétrus Borel, that young poet who seemed so certain to become famous but did not, and through them both Gautier was introduced during the summer of 1829 to the great Victor Hugo himself. If we are to believe Gautier's own account, he was so overcome with timidity that he collapsed on the steps outside Hugo's residence, unable for over an hour to ring the doorbell. But he overcame his shyness, and a few months later he became for a brief period a member of a militant organization with purpose and *esprit de corps*. The story has often been told, but it is one well worth the retelling — the premiere of Victor Hugo's play *Hernani* on February 25, 1830.

II *The Premiere of* Hernani

Ever since the great playwrights of the seventeenth century, Corneille, Molière, and Racine, the theater in France has had immense prestige. But although the Classical Moment, as it has been called, had long ago been relegated to history, mediocre craftsmen continued to grind out pseudo-Racinian dramas well into the nineteenth century. The characters borrowed from classical antiquity or distant cultures spoke in the elegant twelve-syllable alexandrine verse before a minimal décor. The three unities of action, place, and time were still observed. As Gautier recalled, "the Classicists found it all perfectly beautiful; but before these 'masterpieces' their admiration couldn't keep them from stifling a yawn."[9] But new life was in the air. Writing almost a half-century later, Gautier looked back with warm nostalgia to those marvelous days of 1829 and 1830. "The present generations must have difficulty imagining the ferment in our minds at that time. A movement like that of the Renaissance was underway. The sap of new life circulated impetuously. Everything was germinating, budding, exploding all at once. Heady perfume came from flowers; the air was drunk, we were mad with lyricism and art."[10] In this atmosphere of total renovation, even lowly melodramas, such as those written early in the century by Guilbert de Pixérécourt, could play a role in transforming the theater. Stage settings lost their abstract qualities and became "real" countrysides with thatch-roofed huts where an innocent maiden might seek refuge from the villain. The Romantics came to realize that if raised to a higher artistic level, melodrama could serve as a vehicle for their passionate visions. Alexandre Dumas, *père*, had already in February, 1829, written a prose historical melodrama, *Henri III et sa cour* ("Henry III and His Court"), set in the swashbuckling sixteenth century. Death on stage, once proscribed by classical doctrine, now became commonplace, especially with Shakespeare's growing influence on the French theater.

Victor Hugo quickly established himself as the leader of the new group of dramatists. He had already made his mark on the theater not only with *Cromwell* (1827), a play so long that it is only rarely performed, but even more with its preface which demanded the abolition of the unities of time and place and preached, following the Shakespearean example, a mixture of the sublime and the grotesque within a single work. Hugo's disciples swore by this preface, which became a manifesto of the new movement. As Gautier put it, "it shone in our eyes like the Tablets of the Law on Sinai."[11] The young leader's first play to try to reach the stage was *Marion de Lorme* in 1829, but because of its portrayal of a weak king, it incurred the displeasure of the royal censor. Hugo tried again with *Hernani*, a tale which combined lyric love poetry of the highest order with vulgar clowning — a king hides in a closet in a lady's bedroom to avoid scandal. Conservatives were distressed at such innovations and were especially incensed that *Hernani* would be performed at the Théâtre-Français, that bastion of artistic respectability. If they could only pack the theater and hiss the play to death, perhaps upstart Romanticism might be crushed once and for all.

It was then in an atmosphere of glorious conflict that both sides prepared for battle. Gautier's own account of what happened is easily the best record we have of that evening, and we shall let him tell the story directly: "Gérard [de Nerval] was responsible for recruiting young people for this evening which promised to be so stormy. . . . He had in his pocket a bundle of little red squares of paper with the Spanish word *hierro*, meaning iron or steel, marked in a bizarre scrawl in a corner of each ticket. The motto, whose Castillian arrogance was most suited to Hernani's character, meant as well that we must be in our struggle open, brave, and as faithful as a sword."[12] Thus it was that Gautier found himself at the head of a small squad of his own choosing that he brought with him to the theater. Never, he recalled, had he felt such great joy. In order to shock the conservatives the young rebels dressed outlandishly for the occasion. Some wore satin and velvet, sometimes lined with fur. Painters came in artist's smocks. Anything to contrast with the everlasting black dress suit and stovepipe hat of the old habitués. Gautier himself came wearing soft gray trousers set off by a dazzling red (perhaps pink, perhaps crimson; the accounts vary) dress coat faced with black velvet. The legend of the "gilet rouge" became so famous that even today when Gautier's name is mentioned, often the first thing that comes to mind is this flamboyant article of clothing.

The doors to the theater were opened early, six or seven hours before curtain time. The Romantics installed themselves at strategic spots around the hall. If we are to believe Gautier, they ate bread and chocolate, argued literature, demanded aloud the execution of some old fogey. By curtain time, tensions ran high. The orchestra and balcony were "paved with bald academic and classical pates." Then the first line was spoken:

> Serait-ce déjà lui? — C'est bien à l'escalier
> Dérobé . . . .
> (Could that be him already? — I'm sure I hear a noise on the secret stairway)

The audience was startled at finding in a formal tragedy the conscious use of popular language and a daring enjambment which went beyond what was considered proper in the neoclassical tradition. The Classicists were outraged and hissed; the Romantics cheered. It may seem inconceivable that so much ado should be made over so little, but old copies of the play dating from 1830 showed the numerous places where the lines were greeted with whistles and tumult. The play survived its opposition, however, and the Romantics went on to dominate the French theater for the next few years.

If we have dwelt at some length on the premiere of *Hernani*, it is not only because that play marks an important moment in the development of the French theater, but because the evening of February 25, 1830 marked one of the greatest moments of Gautier's life. In fact, if he wrote his *Histoire du romantisme* shortly before he died, it was because he was apparently fearful lest that loyal band of brothers who answered "the call of Hernani's horn" be forgotten. He went on to compare himself and his cohorts to the soldiers of the great Napoleonic armies who in their day had rallied around their leader and then died off one by one.[13] One might point out that at a time when the central personage of this whole affair, Victor Hugo, was looking ahead to what the twentieth century might bring, Théophile Gautier never forgot the glory of this past moment. That soirée was without doubt another of his lost ideal worlds, where heroes are eternally young, brave, and invulnerable, and united in perfect harmony against a common foe. That it was not just an unsubstantial dream conjured from the pages of a book like *Robinson Crusoe* or *Paul et Virginie* but a real event that took place in space and time only made its impact more powerful and more lasting.

III *Le Petit Cénacle*

If Théophile Gautier was ever to succeed as a writer, he had to break the spell of *Hernani* and make his own way. As a consequence, toward the end of 1830 he and several other young writers and artists broke away from the older Romantics and formed their own artistic group (or *cénacle*), meeting regularly at the studio of a young sculptor named Jean Duseigneur. To distinguish their gatherings from those of the first *cénacle* of 1823 which had attracted great figures like Lamartine, Vigny, and Hugo to the home of Charles Nodier, the new generation modestly added the adjective *petit* to the word *cénacle* as if to suggest that they were of lesser stature.

Who were they? What were they like? The host, Jean Duseigneur, added an *h* to his first name so that Jehan would give a flavor of the Middle Ages. The poet Théophile Dondey decided that an anagram of his name, Philothée O'Neddy, sounded more glamorous. There was Joseph Bouchardy, who would become a popular creator of boulevard melodramas, and others, only names to us now, such as Jules Vabre, Célestin Nanteuil, and Auguste Maquet (who loved to anglicize his name to MacKeat, an obscure tribute to Shakespeare's Macbeth, no doubt). Certainly the most colorful of these unknowns was Pétrus Borel, who soon assumed leadership of the group, and by the end of 1832, everyone met at his place. As Gautier remembered him, "his was one of those unforgettable faces. . . young and serious, perfectly regular. His olive skin, gilded with light amber tones as in a painting by an old master, was illuminated by large eyes, shining yet sad, the eyes of an Abencerage thinking of Grenada."[14] Everyone was convinced that Borel would become a great poet, but his talent could not match his presence. Later Gautier was to marvel that he had believed in his genius, and today he is but a footnote to the history of French literature. Gérard de Nerval and Gautier himself were the only members of this coterie to become genuinely important writers.

But even if most of these young men were in fact rather ordinary, Gautier's powerful imagination saw them differently. For him, Pétrus Borel was not the only one to come out of the past from an exotic land like Spain. Gautier felt that Joseph Bouchardy must have been born on the banks of the Indus or the Ganges.[15] He compared Jules Vabre to an American Mohican; Célestin Nanteuil was a refugee from the Middle Ages; Philothée O'Neddy seemed African; and they all called Gautier Othello. Whenever Gautier sought to describe anyone of distinctive bearing, he automatically had recourse to other cultures, especially the more tropical ones. He could never cease longing for his paradise lost.

In such an exotic atmosphere, life was certain to be effervescent. Intoxicated more with art than with wine, they spent hours all talking at once.[16] Despite all their posturing, they were serious about their art. They had been impressed by Hugo's *Les Orientales,* whose preface preached beauty for beauty's sake, and while the future author of *Les Misérables* evolved in the direction of increasing social commitment, for the members of the *petit cénacle,* "the pen, the brush, the lyre, and the sculptor's chisel were [their] only arms, the great masters [their] only gods, and art the only flag which [they] wished to hoist and defend."[17] Even the Revolution of 1830 was less important to them than art. By 1831, as the constitutional monarchy of Louis-Philippe revealed its regressive nature, they did react by moving somewhat to the left. But only Pétrus Borel became truly revolutionary in tone. Curiously, hard work and craftsmanship appealed to the majority of these young men, who were in fact much less wildly extravagant than they appeared. As for Gautier, he would write one antigovernmental satiric poem, "L'Eléphant," but it was for him an exception, not a genuine direction of his talent. Gautier's first poetical work was rather in the tradition of personal Romantic lyricism.

IV *The Early Poetry*

By 1829 Gautier, still only eighteen, had written forty-two individual poems, which were published in July, 1830, by Charles Mary under the title of *Poésies.* The poems were reissued along with some twenty new ones in 1832, and some of these were revised for an 1845 edition of his poetical works.[18] These early efforts are of limited value. On the whole they are obvious imitations of many of the more established Romantic poets of the day, like Sainte-Beuve, Lamartine, and Hugo. The traditional Romantic themes abound. The poet laments the impermanence of life and love, and the theme of death is pervasive. Many poems are set in fall and winter, the seasons of death, and there is even a Hamlet-like meditation upon a skull. It is impossible to be sure whether Gautier believed everything he wrote. The poems sound "insincere," but bad poetry always sounds insincere, and it is in fact likely that these poems represent a mixture of the clichés of the day and the genuine pessimism of a young man seeking in vain some ideal world. The most significant aspect of these early poems is that they are written in a wide variety of verse forms. While these are not new, being largely imitations of those used by Hugo and other poets, they do show Gautier's attempt to find modes of expression that were congenial to his talent. We mentioned above that he had to find his own way and not remain eternally a disciple of the older generation; in fact, it was not long before Gautier became a critic of Romantic excesses.

V *Albertus*

Romanticism offered without any question a vital new means of self-expression that made it a major literary movement. But it also had its ridiculous aspects. If, for instance, the revival of interest in the Middle Ages spoke to modern man's need for a new faith and idealism, it was all too easy for the Gothic cathedral to be overused as an image and to degenerate into a stock cliché. Similarly, *Hamlet* was reduced to a young man brooding over Yorick's skull and meditating on the evanescence of life. Daggers and cloaks, at first symbols of a heroic antibourgeois stance, soon were nothing but Romantic bric-a-brac. The young rebels, then, tended towards a faddish conformism to such an extent that they became vulnerable to satire, and Théophile Gautier was one of the first of the Romantics to take an ironic look at his own enthusiasm.

Albertus, ou l'âme et le péché, légende théologique ("Albertus, or The Soul and Sin, A Theological Legend") was composed in 1831, reworked and republished the following year. It is a narrative poem of one hundred twenty-two stanzas, each consisting of twelve lines of alexandrine (twelve-syllable) verse, except for the last line of each stanza, which is octosyllabic. It tells the story of an ugly witch, Véronique, who is magically transformed (at midnight, of course) into an alluring young woman. The hero, Albertus, is the only man who seems to be indifferent to her. Tanned, yet with an "Italian" pallor, his hair tumbling in disorder, showing a noble brow "whose exterior reveals his inner nature," he is the very model of the Romantic hero of the Byronic type. Eventually, he is lured to the witch's palace, agrees to sell his soul, and makes passionate love to Véronique. But the witch of course resumes her true shape, and Albertus and she ride off on broomsticks to a witches' sabbath conducted by the Devil himself. In the morning the hero's mangled body is found in a clearing.

But the reader should not take the poem at face value. All the "terror" is presented with tongue in cheek. Like Byron in *Don Juan*, Gautier is careful to keep the reader from being caught up in the story by intruding constantly into his tale with every kind of digression. He makes frequent comparisons of the scene he is describing to various paintings, a manner of suggesting that the story is not "real" but derived from artistic and literary traditions. Having made it impossible for the reader to suspend disbelief willingly, to be caught up in the spell that such a story could cast, Gautier further increases the esthetic distance by the use of humor. The following sample is typical. After describing the witch's hovel, Gautier comments:

> En entrant là, Satan, bien qu'hérétique,
> D'épouvante glacé, comme un bon catholique,
> Ferait le signe de la croix. (XII)

(If he entered there, Satan, although a heretic,/Chilled with horror, like a good Catholic/Would cross himself.)

The poet also uses the trick of rhyming words of different languages, a technique that is normally amusing. The painter *Giorgone* rhymes with *prône, diable* with *fashionable, symphonie* with *dilettanti,* much in the manner of Ogden Nash. In short, *Albertus* is in large measure a parody of Romantic literature, especially of tales of the macabre and the supernatural. The witch's hovel comes straight out of Goethe's *Faust;* the name Albertus is borrowed from the Albertus of the Middle Ages to whom were attributed two horrifying books of magic; Hugo's *Notre-Dame de Paris* and Charles Nodier's *Infernalia* furnished other tidbits. There are other sources, Scott and Mérimée among novelists, Musset among the poets. Critics who have objected to Gautier's "excessive" imitation miss the point. Parody requires the presence of all the trappings to be parodied.

While Gautier was enjoying poking fun at Romantic excesses in *Albertus*, once in a while the parody dissolves and Gautier becomes serious despite himself. Occasionally the narrator muses on the nature of sexual attraction. The plot suggests that it leads to self-destruction, but Gautier also notes its positive qualities, feeling that it can create a momentary paradise:

> . . . . moments délicieux,
> Et si longs et si courts qui valent une vie,
> Et que voudrait payer l'Ange qui les envie
> De son éternité de bonheur dans les cieux.
> . . . .
> Amour! le seul péché qui vaille qu'on se damne.

(Delicious moments,/ Long or short, which are worth a whole life,/ And for which the Angel who envies them would gladly pay/ With his eternity of happiness in Heaven./ . . . Love, the only sin worth being damned for.)

But for the most part, *Albertus* remains a delightful spoof and should be appreciated as such. Nor was it to be Gautier's last.

VI *Les Jeunes-France*

On August 30, 1831, — Gautier's twentieth birthday — the newspaper *Le Figaro* took note of the rising young generation of Romantic artists and baptized them the *Jeunes-France*. According to the paper, the group was composed of painters who wrote and poets who painted, of young men who wept over Romantic verse and went into convulsions over "primitive colors." Soon the definition was enlarged to characterize any extreme Romantic posturing. The publisher Eugène Renduel, who had found young Gautier "amusing," suggested that he write "something funny" on this subject,[19] and Gautier, who had already tried his hand with *Albertus*, was ready. As he told it later, his book, *Les Jeunes-France: romans goguenards* ("The Jeunes-France: Tales Told with Tongue in Cheek"), was a "kind of *Précieuses ridicules* of Romanticism," referring to Molière's play that mocked seventeenth-century preciosity. The volume appeared in August, 1833.

In actual fact, there is much more to *Les Jeunes-France* than a satire of Romanticism, and we shall have occasion to examine these other matters in the next chapter. But the volume does include in three of its six pieces of prose fiction a delightful parody of Romantic excesses. The first of these is "Daniel Jovard ou la conversion d'un Classique." Jovard, as a name, is close to the slang word, *jobard*, which means sucker, a fact that Gautier points out at the beginning of the story. The narrative chronicles a young provincial writer's experience when he arrives in the capital and encounters the new Romanticism. An ordinary youth, he wears conservative clothes, accepts rather traditional Voltairean politics, and in literature, he is a resolute neo-classical poet, writing such horrors as:

> Quel transport m'agite, et quel est mon délire!
> Un souffle a fait vibrer les cordes de ma lyre.
> O Muses, chastes soeurs, et toi, grand Apollon,
> Daignez guider mes pas dans le sacré vallon!

Our wretched translation of this doggerel only does the text justice:

> What ecstasy disturbs me, and what is this holy fire?
> A breath has caused to quiver the strings upon my lyre.
> O Muses, chaste sisters, and thou, Apollo, hail!
> Deign to guide my steps into the sacred vale!

But fortunately, or perhaps unfortunately, the budding poet meets an old acquaintance who converts him to the new cause. Ferdinand explains to Daniel that it is not hard to learn to be a Romantic. Just as in cooking there are recipes, to write a Romantic book, "you take a couple of loose sheets and write a preface and a postface, you assume a nom-de-plume, you say you died of consumption or that you've blown your brains out; then you serve it all up piping hot and you're an instant success."[20] The mentor adds that "you must be careful about your epigraphs. Put some in English, German, Spanish and Arabic. If you can manage one in Chinese, it can have a tremendous effect." Ferdinand also teaches his pupil to look vaguely like a refugee from the Middle Ages and to use all the "in" artistic terms. So Daniel, converted, goes home and burns his collection of Classical authors, dresses in "Romantic" fashion, and grows a goatee. He learns to be "dreamy, intimate, artistic, fated, or even like Dante" (p. 89), and he learns all this in one morning. Now our hero can rhyme richly and break up the alexandrine line of verse. He shaves off some of his hair, creating a very noble brow, in an attempt to emulate Victor Hugo, whom he now adores. His poetry changes radically as well. From the stilted neo-classicism of his earlier effort he moves to the frantic and macabre:

> Par l'enfer! je me sens un immense désir
> De broyer sous mes dents sa chair, et de saisir
> Avec quelque lambeau de sa peau bleue et verte,
> Son coeur demi-pourri dans sa poitrine ouverte.

which we make so bold as to render:

> By the fiends! I feel in me an immense craving
> To crunch her flesh with my teeth and, raving,
> To seize with a strip of her blueish-green breast
> Her half-rotted heart in her ripped-open chest.

In another selection, "Elias Wildmanstadius, ou l'homme du moyen âge," Gautier provides us with more fanciful details about a young Romantic. This "man from the Middle Ages" lives, at least mentally, in the idealized world of illuminated manuscripts and heroic jousting. Elias' house dates from the sixteenth century, a bit modern perhaps, but at least it has cracks in its damp, oozing stone walls. And he delights in the ogival windows, with their lozenge-shaped panes set in leaden cames. His speech is so studded with archaisms that he is incomprehensible. The poor young man dies suddenly at the very moment that the cathedral is struck by lightning.

Perhaps the high point of Gautier's satire is his story "Le Bol de punch." The *Jeunes-France* often enjoyed drinking punch which, with some strong spirits on top, could be made to burn with a mephistophelic blue flame. Expense, rather than Satanism, may actually explain the popularity of this drink, for a bowl could be purchased for twelve or thirteen *sous*. But whether out of impish humor or swaggering bravado, the *Jeunes-France* gave the impression that the punch was the culmination of unspeakable orgies, and indeed, Gautier discovered the phrase *wild orgy (orgie échevelée)* in four different contemporary works — by Honoré de Balzac, Jules Janin, P.-L. Jacob, and Eugène Sue. Gautier's clever idea was to imagine an orgy based on a literary account. According to the plot, the *Jeunes-France* divide themselves into four groups to act out the four texts, and then hold an orgy that follows the scripts meticulously, as if to anticipate Oscar Wilde's famous dictum that Life imitates Art. As, of course, life and literature tend to be widely at variance, the young men find it difficult to relive in fact what had been told in fiction. "Le Bol de punch" is a lively spoof, still fun to read today.

VII *The Impasse du Doyenné*

The *petit cénacle* did not last past the first months of 1833. Another momentary paradise vanished like a mirage as diverging interests destroyed the group's precarious unity. But dissolution did not, even yet, end Gautier's carefree years. As luck would have it, in late 1834, Gautier's father was transferred to Passy, then a village on the outskirts of Paris. Gautier, eager for independence, and unwilling to spend hours commuting to where his friends lived, remained behind in the city.

His closest friend, Gérard de Nerval, had already found lodgings near the Louvre. The area was almost a slum, but it held no terrors for a gathering of young men dedicated to art. Nerval shared rooms here with Camille Rogier, and soon others joined them, and not only Gautier. There was Arsène Houssaye, who would one day become the director of the Théâtre-Français, and whose *Confessions* recall in engaging fashion the communal life in the Impasse du Doyenné. Célestin Nanteuil and Auguste Maquet, holdovers from the *petit cénacle,* transferred their residences there. Others, including giants like Eugène Delacroix and Alexandre Dumas, stayed there briefly. The painters painted and the writers wrote, but the writers could paint, too, and the artists enjoyed poetry. They gave parties, and if money was short, they improvised. On one occasion, they each painted a mural scene to decorate the walls of the room. Of course there were women there. We know that Gérard de Nerval was, in the words of René Jasinski, "haunted by the actress Jenny Colon."[21] Arsène Houssaye had the very tangible Ninon, and Rogier a girl they called "La Cydalise." She was thin and wan, the very picture of a Romantic heroine, and she was even suffering from tuberculosis. Gautier fell in love with her, but after a few months she resolved the triangle by dying. Gautier was apparently deeply touched by the memory of this girl, for years later in a nostalgic poem, "Le Château du souvenir" ("The Castle of Memory"), he evoked her sad, delicate charm. There was another, more strapping girl called Victorine, with whom Gautier had a passionate affair. The wonderful months spent in the Impasse du Doyenné, where they lived "like Robinson Crusoes," marked the last of Gautier's truly idyllic existences. He summed it up with the following lyrical apostrophe: "O happy time when we became drunk with youth on only a glass of water, when we thought we were Don Juans because the girl in the attic room next door smiled at us through the mignonettes and the sweet peas! What wonderful dreams we dreamed, wreathed in tobacco smoke! What great poetry we recited, what wonderful paintings we saw. . . ."[22] No wonder, then, that those months spent there, as well as the premiere of *Hernani*, loomed so large in Gautier's memory for the rest of his life.

But no paradise can last forever in the real world. First, writing was becoming for Gautier a time-consuming way of life. There were critical articles (1834 - 35), which would later be published as *Les Grotesques* (1844), and *Mademoiselle de Maupin* and its preface (1835 - 36). Besides these major productions, there were minor efforts written for short-lived literary magazines. In 1836 Gautier went to work on a regular basis as the art and theater critic for the paper *La Presse*. He had to do so, for by now he had met Eugénie Fort, a woman of whom we know little, and had had a child by her, Théophile Gautier, junior, whom he legally recognized. For our author, carefree youth — what Joanna Richardson calls his "green season"[23] — was over. Henceforth he was a professional writer. Fortunately, the fictional and poetic worlds of Gautier's maturity would have a permanence that life in the *petit cénacle* and the Impasse du Doyenné could not have. For Gautier, as would be the case for Gustave Flaubert, art was the one means of preserving the ideal, of overcoming decay and dissolution. For Gautier, it was, in a sense, salvation, the one means by which he could overcome the tyranny of time and finitude.

CHAPTER 2

The Road to Mademoiselle de Maupin

I *Romantic Dualism*

THE split in personality that made it difficult for Gautier to harmonize the ideal and the real was hardly unique with him. In fact, it has been widespread enough to achieve theological expression. Gnostic or Manichean thought sees man radically split between soul and body. The soul desires the infinite, but the corrupt body keeps it prisoner. This view of man had its origins in early Eastern thought, but it soon penetrated into Western Europe. It was perhaps strongest during the Middle Ages, but it has continued until modern times. In the seventeenth century, Descartes, for example, used the division of body and soul as a starting point for his proof of the existence of God. If certain eighteenth-century rationalists tried to resolve the tension by explaining all human phenomena in terms of the material body and refused to take the idea of the soul seriously, the Romantic reaction against purely rationalistic thought gave Manichean dualism a new vigor, for the Romantics were keenly aware of their mortality, and yet at the same time were penetrated by a feeling of quasi-divinity. Lamartine put it the most succinctly in his *Méditations poétiques:*

> Borné dans sa nature, infini dans ses voeux;
> L'Homme est un Dieu tombé qui se souvient des cieux.
> ("L'Homme")

(Limited by his nature, infinite in his desires;/Man is a fallen God who remembers Heaven. — "Man")

Nor was this statement unique among writers of that generation. To take but two examples among many, George Sand was to write in *Lélia* (1833): "Limited beings, we try ceaselessly to ignore the insatiable desires which consume us,"[1] and Victor Hugo incorporated the idea into his preface to *Cromwell.* "Christianity," he wrote, "teaches man that he has two lives to lead, one ephemeral, the other immortal; one is of the earth, the other of heaven. It teaches him that he is dual as is his destiny, that there is in him an animal and an intelligence, a body and a soul."[2]

This sense of a dual being caused the Romantics considerable strain. They found human finitude intolerable, but divinity impossible. They could no more abandon their dreams of the absolute, however, than they could shuck off their humanity. But to leave the division between the two halves of their selves unhealed was painful, and so they were forever moving back and forth between these two polarities or making unsuccessful efforts to reconcile the two. This problem of a divided personality explains, incidentally, better than any revolt against Classicism, the obsessive antitheses of Victor Hugo. In similar manner, Vigny's Samson, Moses, and Jesus all feel this same uncertainty concerning their nature. Perhaps the best example of this dichotomy in Gautier's early poetry comes from "L'Oiseau captif" ("The Caged Bird"). Its key stanza compares the bird to his own soul:

> Mon âme est comme toi: de sa cage mortelle
> Elle s'ennuie, hélas! et souffre, et bat de l'aile.
> Ange elle-même, suivre un ange Ithuriel,
> S'enivrer d'infini, d'amour, et de lumière,
> Et de remonter à la cause première.

(My soul is like you; with its mortal cage/ It is bored, alas! and suffers, and beats its wings./ An angel itself, it longs to follow an angel Ithuriel,/ To be drunk on infinity, love, and light,/ And eager to go back up to the origin of creation.)

II *Five Short Stories*

In the previous chapter we discussed several stories from *Les Jeunes-France* as parodies of Romanticism but indicated that the volume was of interest in other ways as well. In another of these tales, "Onuphrius," the hero is a painter who, because he is an artist, is eager to achieve perfect expression of his ideal vision, but he is constantly frustrated because he falls short of his goal. Unable to cope with the tension, Onuphrius loses his hold on reality and soars into the ideal realms of the imagination. Ultimately he goes mad and is destroyed. No wonder the image of Icarus is often used to describe the Romantic artists.[3]

"Onuphrius" deals with a painter wrestling with his art, but in other stories we find the protagonist searching for the ideal, not in art, but in women. He either hesitates between two women, sensing that to choose only one will leave his desires but half satisfied, or else having chosen one, wishes he could change and choose the other. The first story of *Les Jeunes-France*, "Sous la table" ("Under the Table") shows the pattern in clear if elementary form. The story was borrowed from Alfred de Musset's "Suzon" (1831), but the fact that Gautier chose it makes it significant in any event. The plot is simple enough: Two drunken young men grumble at the shortcomings of their mistresses. One of the girls is straightforward, but unexciting, with no interest in extravagant pleasures. The other is just the opposite, sensuous, wild, and expensive. One is too little, the other too much. So the young men agree to a swap. A month later they are just as dissatisfied and "solve" their problem by staying drunk all the time.

Another story, not in *Les Jeunes-France*, but taken from a small collection of tales called *Contes humoristiques* ("Humorous Stories") is called, rather significantly, "Laquelle des deux: histoire perplexe" ("Which One of the Two: A Perplexing Tale"). Dating from 1833, it tells of a young man attracted to two sisters, one blond, the other brunette. The two girls are always together, which fact causes considerable annoyance to any young man in love with either one. The hero hesitates between the two and ultimately discovers that separately they please him less than when he sees them together. He achieves a few moments of genuine happiness when he takes the hands of both girls in his and kisses them simultaneously. The story ends with the hero's departure and the banal marriages of the girls to other men. Preposterous as the story is, it shows through its allegory the narrator's need to unite the blond and the brunette, that is, the ideal and the real, into one. The lesson is apparently that such unity can only be fleeting and partial.

Gautier attacked the same subject in another of his tales from *Les Jeunes-France*, entitled "Celle-ci et Celle-là" ("This One and That One"). Curiously, this story is very little known except to specialists, but it is of the greatest importance to anyone interested in Gautier. It suggests a genuine solution to his dilemma, for it is only superficially a satire of the young Romantic in love. We have a hero, Rodolphe, who decides that he needs a towering passion to fill his life and that only an Italian or Spanish lady will do. It is true that he has a servant girl, Mariette, who frequently shares his bed, but for Rodolphe, the relationship is merely carnal and convenient, totally lacking the transcendent ideal that can appeal to his most sublime aspirations. One evening at the opera he sees the woman of his dreams: mysterious, exciting, and definitely Italian. But, alas, disillusionment is not long in setting in. It turns out that she is not from Italy, but from Château-Thierry, and to a Parisian, Château-Thierry is about as romantic as is Bridgeport to a New Yorker. Worse yet, he has already composed a poem whose opening line ends in "Italienne," and now he must replace the word. Calling on Madame de M***, and eventually getting her alone, he finds her resistance to be nonexistent. Thus he cannot even use frustration to heighten his passion. To add to his woes, her husband is blind or complaisant. A denunciatory anonymous letter sent him by Rodolphe himself in an effort to create a dramatic confrontation has no effect. The husband refuses to believe it. In short, the whole affair degenerates into utter banality. Meanwhile, Mariette announces that she is leaving her master. Truly in love with him, she has suffered intensely from jealousy at his conquest of the dark "Italian." She has lost her gaiety and the bloom is gone from her cheeks. Rodolphe becomes aware of her pallor and her sorrowful eyes, and as he has a Romantic esthetic, he takes a renewed interest in her. Not realizing what has happened to Rodolphe's "ideal" love affair, she refuses and announces resolutely: "I cannot, as you do, split my love in half: a soulful love for one girl and a bodily love for the other. I love you with body and soul, and I want to be loved in the same way."[4] The rhetoric of the text makes it clear that she is wise to refuse any dualism, and so the hero learns his lesson. Through her he comes to realize that "there is more true passion in this girl than in twenty simpering idiots of the other type" (p. 193). At this point, Albert, a friend of Rodolphe's, enters to conclude: "O my friend! one must be crazy to leave home in the hope of finding poetry. Poetry is no more here than there, for it is within us. There are those who seek inspiration at the ends of the earth, and cannot realize that within a few miles of Paris they have what they were looking for. . . . Poetry is everywhere" (pp. 194 - 95).

Having finished the narrative, the author intrudes to inform us that the story was actually an allegory: "Rodolphe, uncertain, drifting, full of vague desires, seeking beauty and passion, represents the inexperienced, youthful human soul; Madame de M*** represents classical poetry, beautiful and cold, dazzling and false, similar in every way to ancient statues, goddesses without a heart. . . . Moreover, she is available to all, easy to touch, despite her pretentions and her haughty airs. Mariette is true poetry, without corset or makeup, a likeable girl, suitable for an artist . . . who is alive with life. . . . M. de M*** is heavy common sense, stupid prose . . . married to false poetry" (p. 199). The conclusion to this story goes beyond Gautier's own explanation, however, to suggest that genuine success, whether in love or in art, must come through confronting the real, not the illusory or the artificial. In that way one achieves unity of being. But a truth stated is not a lesson deeply learned, as Gautier's life reveals. In the Impasse du Doyenné, he needed the vigorous, passionate Victorine to complement the delicate Cydalise, and the fact that the poet never married can probably best be explained in the same way. He would no doubt have felt it an irrevocable choice that would not permit him to shift to a different woman once he had become dissatisfied with the incompleteness of his wife. Gautier's art reflects his psychology. In his fiction — with the exception of Rodolphe of "Celle-ci et celle-là" — his heroes continually try to reconcile opposites but do not succeed very well. If we look ahead to a story written in 1839, we find one of the most clear-cut examples of this attempt and failure at integration of ideal and real.

"La Toison d'or" ("The Golden Fleece"), was inspired by Gautier's visit to the Low Countries in 1836 in the company of Gérard de Nerval. Gautier explained that his goal was to see whether the local girls could live up to the excellence of Rubens' paintings of them,[5] and in the Cathedral in Antwerp he saw a Rubens painting which provided him with the nucleus for a short story. The hero, Tiburce, a painter and poet (like Gautier), has gone to the Low Countries in search of a blond mistress of the Rubens type. While in Antwerp, dissatisfied with all the real women he has seen, he falls in love with a blond Mary Magdalene in a Rubens painting. But although her perfection makes mere mortal women seem uninteresting, he is aware that it is difficult to make love to a painting and that he has, after all, come there for a mistress. Eventually he does find a girl, similar in appearance to the blonde in the painting, less perfect, of course, but more tangible. Torn between the ideal and the real, Tiburce has difficulty choosing. The story ends with the girl becoming his model as well as his mistress, thus permitting him to eat his cake and paint it too. But the final synthesis is only a superficial reconciliation, a trick to cover up the basic fact that he — and through him Gautier — cannot choose. So although the lesson that Mariette gave Rodolphe offered a real solution, "La Toison d'or" reveals that Gautier did not evolve in this direction but reverted once more to the split between his two extremes. It should therefore come as no surprise to discover that this obsessive unresolved problem is at the heart of one of Gautier's best known works, and the one which made his reputation — *Mademoiselle de Maupin*.

III Mademoiselle de Maupin

In September 1833, still enjoying the success of *Les Jeunes-France*, Gautier signed a contract to write an historical romance based on the life of Madelaine de Maupin. No doubt his publisher, Eugène Renduel, was hoping for a best seller, for historical romances had become popular in France, thanks to the influence of Sir Walter Scott. Alfred de Vigny, Honoré de Balzac, and Victor Hugo had already done well with *Cinq-Mars*, *Les Chouans*, and *Notre-Dame de Paris*, and Gautier's subject seemed even more promising from a commercial point of view, for this incredible seventeenth-century woman was the perfect choice for an adventure tale. She was not only a professional singer, she was also a first-rate swordsman, often went about disguised as a man, and had flamboyant love affairs with representatives of both sexes. The story goes that she even set fire to a convent as part of a plot to run off with some girl. Having later turned to religion, she died, apparently repentant, in a convent, at the ripe young age of thirty.

But anyone familiar with the story knows that Gautier's finished work[6] did not turn out to be a sparkling adventure tale that combined in delicious fashion the morally edifying and the taboo. At this point in his life Gautier was too obsessed with his problem of identity to submit himself to telling with the necessary detachment a complex historical tale with multiple characters of different types. His preference was, as we have seen, to use techniques of allegory to represent different intellectual or existential positions and then to set the characters against each other. That is why his characters, incidentally, seem rather two-dimensional and unreal. Allegory normally produces this impression. So, as he did with his short stories, Gautier ignored the rich historical possibilities of his subject and reduced the plot to a simple geometrical triangle: a hero, Albert, and his mistress, Rosette, both in love with the exquisite Madelaine de Maupin, who is disguised as a young man Théodore. Eventually her true sex is revealed, she makes love during one long night to each of the other two in turn and then disappears forever. But this skeleton of a plot is submerged under lyrical outpourings of thoughts and feelings of a Romantic kind. Without a sustained, suspenseful plot, the book sold badly, and the disgusted Renduel turned his back on Gautier and refused to have anything more to do with him.

If it was out of the question, then, to judge *Maupin* as an historical romance, how could it be viewed? Schoolboys read it in secret for a few salacious passages, but the prevalent attitude of the nineteenth century was to refuse to examine it at all. Instead, contemporaries concentrated on its famous preface that preached Art for Art's sake through its dictum that "everything useful is ugly." But René Jasinski has shown in detail that the preface was written in response to pressures of government censorship that plagued young writers of the early 1830's and that it has practically no connection with the fiction. If preface and story were published together, it was only to make enough total pages to fill out a two-volume edition.[7] As a consequence, the preface is of little value in clarifying the nature of the story, and we shall therefore postpone discussion of it until our next chapter, which deals with Gautier's criticism.

There has been some commentary treating the fiction itself, but usually only to condemn it as an incoherent structure and to urge that we limit ourselves to enjoying a few lyrical bits and pieces. A typical judgment is that of Adolphe Boschot, who wrote in the introduction to his edition of *Maupin*: "This seductive but composite book in no way resembles a carefully constructed work put together by a specialist. And it's a good thing too. *Maupin* is a book full of fantasies, an assemblage of lyrical bits, of confidences, dreams and bravura couplets" (pp. xxiv - xxv).

Eventually, however, nearly all critics have agreed on the main value of the text. They assure us that the hero, Albert, is Gautier himself, and hence the importance of *Maupin* is to provide us with information about the author through a direct examination of the "fictional" hero. But autobiography and a partially autobiographical piece of prose fiction are not identical and must not be treated as if they were. To use a directly biographical approach raises an awkward question: if Albert *is* Gautier, who are Rosette and Madelaine? Their identity becomes a problem, for if they, too, are not biographical, the relationship with Albert becomes fiction, and Albert would then no longer be Gautier. So, inevitably, critics have linked Gautier's mistresses with the former, and George Sand's name has been suggested for the latter.[8] But George Sand has never been amorously linked to Gautier, and his mistresses did not fit the character of Rosette very well. Albert Smith has been the only critic to sense that this approach can be abused and to warn against seeing *Maupin* as "psychic autobiography."[9] Yet if it is wise to caution against oversimplified biographical criticism, it cannot be denied that Gautier put much of himself into the character of Albert. To understand the importance of the author's presence in the text requires an explanation of the basic structure of the entire work.

Maupin consists of seventeen chapters, most of which constitute letters written either by Albert or by Madelaine to absent friends or to each other. Of these, the first five are somewhat special. Consisting of the hero's lyrical outpouring to an invisible Silvio, they seem to have only the remotest connection with the action that follows. There are no references to any details of seventeenth-century life; on the contrary, there are even minor anachronisms, for the narrator has most of the characteristics and even the language of an early nineteenth-century Romantic. It is true that Rosette is introduced and that she remains important throughout the fiction, but these first five letters, which constitute nearly one-third of the entire work, almost give the impression of having been composed earlier, set aside, and then adapted to the story of Théodore-Madelaine. Gautier did state that he wrote *Maupin* uninterruptedly from beginning to end, but scholars have been unanimous in judging his comment unreliable,[10] although as the manuscript has long since disappeared, final proof of an hypothesis of this kind is lacking.

If, as many suspect, the first part was written separately, then it is likely that Gautier was writing some kind of personal confession in fictional guise. This literary form, the confession, was popular among the Romantics, and had been since Jean-Jacques Rousseau. Constant's *Adolphe* (1816) and Musset's *Les Confessions d'un enfant du siècle* (1836) are but two of the best known of such efforts. At any rate, we do know that Albert was the titular hero of the "theological legend," *Albertus*; his name cropped up as one of the characters in "Le Bol de punch," and he is some kind of authorial spokesman in "Celle-ci et celle-là." To move to Gautier's life, we know that he was often called Albert during the days of the *petit cénacle*. There is, then, similarity between the two, but there is not identity. The similarity is that Albert's problem is the same as Gautier's; the difference is that while Gautier was a normally complex human being with different interests and activities, Albert represents only one aspect of his creator's nature. Gautier has simplified him for the purpose of his demonstration.

IV *The Characters: Albert and Rosette*

Albert, as we said above, quickly reveals himself as a typical Romantic. He moans that he can touch his horizons in every direction (p. 42), that he has bursts of energy but no goals (p. 43), that he desires nothing because he desires everything (p. 45). He is in love with the impossible; he feels himself to be above ordinary men and even wishes he could be a god (p. 141). All this reminds one of Chateaubriand's René. Of course, he would prefer to have his dreams of the ideal become concrete and accessible, and so we find him talking like Tiburce of "La Toison d'or," hoping that one of Raphaël's virgins will step down from her canvas and kiss him (p.45). Like Gautier, Albert wants to have the ideal and the real, but as the character in a painting must remain on the canvas, he accepts, because he must, a lesser goal, Rosette. He calls her Rosette because she was wearing a pink dress when he first met her, as if to suggest that for him she is her body and exterior garments. He finds her beautiful and charming, witty and sensual, but lacking in total sublimity. Yet, despite her supposed limitations, she has a remarkable effect on the hero. "She is the only woman with whom I have been able to be truly myself, and I am fatuous enough to believe that I've never been so keen. . . . My mind has opened up in total freedom, and by the skill and fire of her conversation, she has made me find more intelligence in myself than I thought I had and than perhaps I really did have" (p. 87). He confesses further: "She is so 'right' in her environment that one has no desire to leave it to go soaring off into the clouds." She fills "real life" for him, and he sees her as a perfect incarnation of "veritable truth" *(la vérité vraie;* p. 241).

Despite his disclaimers, she does not fill his life completely and he does desire to soar into the clouds. He admits that he is an utter idiot who is never satisfied and who goes around seeking the impossible (pp. 87 - 88). In a moment of lucidity, he realizes that his nature is dualistic and that like oil and water the two parts of his self constantly separate. These two parts are, of course, his soul and his body, and as in "L'Oiseau captif," his soul is a prisoner of his carnal form (p. 94). In short, Albert is another incarnation not only of Tiburce but of Rodolphe of "Celle-ci et celle-là" and, less directly, of the unnamed hero of "Laquelle des deux."

As for Rosette, we must be on guard lest we believe everything Albert says about her, for the hero is not a fully reliable narrator. In the equilibrium of the narrative she turns out to be more than mere body and pleasure, just as did Mariette of "Celle-ci et celle-là." She is a real person, not a sex object, and she can suffer keenly when the great love she seeks passes her by. She has a fine intelligence which has no trouble in fathoming Albert's nature. She says of him later to Madelaine de Maupin: "I was a means for him, not a goal. . . . Something attracts him and calls irresistibly to him which is not of this world" (p. 155). She is, in short, a person who has achieved her wisdom, insight, and love, not in opposition to her carnal reality, but by accepting and developing it. In so doing, she has managed to avoid Albert's dualism and has integrated body and psyche in a wholeness of human personality. Albert, however, does not dare — or is unable — to descend into the complexity of human reality. "I tried to go down into her heart, but I always stopped on the top step" (pp. 95 - 96).

Thus two positions have been taken: a longing for perfection (Albert) and an acceptance of the riches of imperfect human life (Rosette). Which of the two is normative for the text? Biographical critics have automatically assumed that Albert speaks for the author, but the hero's personality and philosophical stance are hardly to be preferred to Rosette's charm and ability to bring out the best in others, even in a permanent adolescent like Albert. After all, Mariette, who represented reality in "Celle-ci et celle-là," was superior in wisdom to Rodolphe. To resolve this question for *Maupin,* we must turn to our third principal character, the titular heroine herself.

V *The Characters: Madelaine*

The problem with the heroine is that she exists on two entirely different, and even antithetical planes. She is some kind of allegorical figure, representing perfect beauty, but she is also presented as a human being with human characteristics. This dual nature explains why on the one hand to Georges Poulet she is the concrete form of Albert's ideal dream,[11] and on the other hand to Albert Smith, she is a character in her own right.[12] Let us consider each in turn.

The short stories that we treated in the first part of this chapter all revolve around two subjects: women and art. Furthermore, the two tend to blend into each other. Mariette represents true poetry, and Tiburce falls in love with a painting. The reason Gautier combines the two is that behind his musings on art and love is a deep desire for true beauty. Hence, not only art but also women are often for him the means of achieving this transcendent end. This idea comes out clearly in *Maupin*. Albert, speculating on his attraction to women, eventually confesses that mind and soul in a woman are secondary. All that he insists on is physical beauty (p. 133). This thought, expressed in the text many times in one form or another, provides Albert with an easy transition to philosophizing on the nature of beauty itself. First, he tries to avoid taking an idealistic position, claiming that beauty is not absolute but only relative (p. 64). But if it is not absolute, he asks, where does the concept of its absoluteness come from? Remarkably, he blames it all on great artists, who have by the beauty of their painting inculcated the concept into us. Apparently he does not stop to consider that there is a tradition, at least as old as Plato, which considers objects in this world as reflecting an abstract perfection on high. Although on one occasion Albert does try to make fun of Platonism, cynically using it to seduce a woman who likes her carnal realities clothed in lofty ideals, he is without question a kind of Platonist himself. He confesses: "I adore above all else the beauty of form; — beauty for me is Divinity made visible, happiness made tangible, it is heaven descended to earth," a remark that leads to his conclusion that beauty is the "pure personification of the thought of God" (pp. 133 - 34). This abstract purity, Albert tells us, takes its ultimate human form in the figure of the hermaphrodite. This idea is, of course, traditional, reaching back at least to Classical times. The essential idea is that beauty is harmony and completeness, and since the masculine and feminine principles are incomplete separately, their union in one form represents a metaphor for totality and perfection. Gautier in his turn adopts the same image. We know that he was attracted by the slightly androgynous grace of the dancer Fanny Elssler, and in a later poem, "Contralto," he admires a voice that can be either female or male. If Winckelmann, the German art historian who perhaps suggested the image to Gautier,[13] sees the androgyne as a feminized young man, Gautier reverses the idea. His hermaphrodite, his ideal of beauty in *Maupin*, is a woman disguised as a man. In a perceptive article Pierre Albouy has had no difficulty showing that Gautier's hermaphrodite is not a true one like Plato's, but hermaphroditic only on some symbolic plane, for her body is amply feminine.[14] Hence, for Albouy, she is an "impossible contradition."[15] The contradition is, of course, but another way of saying that to unite an allegory of abstract perfection with a truly human character in a piece of fiction is not only unwise, it is unworkable.

Gautier did, however, also try to make his heroine a real person, and within the context of the narrative she exists as one. Albert Smith sees her as a real person and describes her as having a split personality, torn as she is between a desire to find a man who incarnates her ideal on the one hand, and her baser human desires on the other.[16] We must agree with this view up to a point, for in letters to a friend that recapitulate her early adolescence, she tells of her longings for perfection in love and her desire to find a man of perfect character to love her perfectly. Suspicious lest she be deceived by reality, she leaves home disguised as a young man in order to mingle with the opposite sex in an effort to find out if men are sincere when they make protestations of eternal love. It does not take her long to discover that their pretty speeches are merely vulgar techniques of seduction. Even more appalling to her, however, is the discovery when sharing a bed in a tavern with a drunken young gentleman, that she is sexually aroused by his presence and feels herself wanting to be made love to, even though they are both dressed. So much for the possibility of achieving perfection, she muses. "Ah! One tries in vain to spread one's wings, they are weighed down by too much slime, the body anchors the soul to earth" (p. 228).

But this sense of division between body and soul, what Professor Smith calls her split personality, is not something given from the beginning. Nor does it remain static. She started with one view and through the impact of the experience at the inn moved to a newer understanding. In contrast to Albert and Rosette, who represent fixed characters, underneath Madelaine's surface perfectionism, something is subtly and at first almost invisibly changing, like snow melting under a crust in late winter. If we look closely we can see that Madelaine belongs more to the tradition of the *Bildungsroman*, for she is truly a character in transition. Next we note that she begins to question ideal perfection itself, as she comes to sense that if one ever should reach the blue horizon of the ideal, one would find there only bare, cracked clay (p. 340). She tries, therefore, to accommodate herself to reality. Her first step is to limit her perfectionism to the body: "If I cannot have a virtuous soul, I would at least like an exquisitely perfect figure," and she too begins to talk about the perfection of the Greek androgyne. At this stage in her evolution she is about on a level with Albert. She senses that she has already moved a considerable distance: "I had come down from the sublime clouds, not all the way to the street and the gutter, but onto a hill of medium height, accessible, although a bit steep." But then her evolution takes another significant step in an attempt to avoid having a perfect body out of harmony with a corrupt soul: "So that my flesh won't lord it over my soul, I wish to sully it as well," and then she moves another step ahead with the sudden thought: "if it is after all sullying it any more than eating or drinking is, — which I doubt" (p. 357). While she still reverts on occasion to the language of perfection, underneath she is basically learning to be human. Now she wishes not the absolute, but happiness, which she defines in a more mature manner as "to be able to develop oneself freely in every way and to become all that one can be." She has arrived finally at a position close to that represented by Rosette. They both wish to be fully realized and integrated human beings.

Because Madelaine is beautiful and honest, and because she is also the titular heroine of Gautier's story, the reader comes to feel in the latter stages of the narrative that she is closer to representing truth than is Albert. With her new-found acceptance of life, she can, like Rosette, now enrich the lives of others. She comes to Albert's room to make him happy by loving him. In so doing, she even pokes fun at his sense of the absolute (which had once been her sense also), telling him that she would have had no trouble in making him believe that she was outraged by his declaration of love and "all your Platonic sighs and your most quintessential gibberish would not have been enough to get me to pardon you for an act that I was actually delighted to accomplish with you" (p. 363). And in terms that accept her human finitude, she adds that she expects from him no oath of eternal love, and she will give him none either, and when his love dies, she will *not* call him a perfidious wretch, and she asks him to spare her similar abuse should she leave him. The evolution of her character is now completed. She has indeed come a long way.

VI *The Conclusion*

We stated at the beginning that the meaning of *Maupin* could not be determined from the preface or from any other exterior evidence, that it is wiser to seek the intent of the text. In this regard, we have been trying to show that, whatever may have been Gautier's desire, the work itself more than suggests a criticism of perfection up to this point, which is seven pages from the end of the entire work. The text indicates a preference for Rosette's rich humanity and Madelaine's new-found understanding over ideals of perfection of character or even of body. The logical outcome should therefore be either Albert's conversion to a less Romantic view or some tragic ending caused by his stubborn adherence to impossible infinities.

But art is a mysterious and unpredictable creation that has been known to escape the control of its originator. Pirandello's *Six Characters in Search of an Author* is only the most famous and dramatic example of the idea that a text — or characters in a text — may escape authorial control and take on a life of their own. We mention this curious phenomenon because it looks very much as if something similar happened to Gautier's story. His text systematically condemns dreams of perfection, but for Gautier to condemn the absolute was to repudiate part of his own being. As we saw in the story "La Toison d'or," he needed the absolute as much as he needed human reality. So, as if suddenly becoming conscious of the fact that in *Maupin* reality was overwhelming the ideal, he created, whether consciously or unconsciously we shall never know, a final brief chapter in which he clumsily undid Madelaine's evolution and desperately reversed the direction of his story. He created a night of incredibly perfect and perfectly incredible love-making. Then, after bestowing the ultimate in sexuality on both Albert and Rosette as a farewell gift, Madelaine leaves forever. Her act perhaps makes sense for Albert, who could never get beyond dreaming anyway, but it is no favor to Rosette, who wanted a real human love within finite human time with a young "man" named Théodore. Gautier's reversal of direction becomes particularly evident when in a note that Madelaine leaves for Albert, she declares in the most absolutist terms that she will never sleep with another man. In short, after having shown her slowly abandoning impossible absolutes, Gautier contradicts himself and reinstates them for her. With his authorial intrusion, he was apparently trying to put both his polarities back into balance. But if the synthesis of "La Toison d'or" is inauthentic, this one is even more so. We are forced to conclude that Gautier's need for an absolute was so great that he was willing to sacrifice not only his character's wholeness of personality for it, but even the integrity of his work of art.

A final comment on *Maupin* is in order. If Gautier refused to move in the direction that seemed so promising in "Celle-ci et celle-là," it was very likely because he did not believe it possible to create an integrated human psyche, for just after Madelaine had reached her final conclusion that happiness is to be able to develop oneself freely in every way, to be all that one can be, she adds ruefully: "But that is impossible, and there is no point in thinking about it" (p. 353). This fundamental pessimism about human identity is the real message of *Maupin*, and perhaps of the entire Romantic age.

CHAPTER 3

Gautier the Critic

As is obvious from the preceding chapters, Théophile Gautier possessed real literary gifts, even if during the decade of the 1830's his works were often imperfect. But Gautier's psychology was not oriented uniquely toward original creation. Baudelaire once remarked that "it was odd to note how easily [Gautier's] curiosity could be aroused and how eagerly he liked to scrutinize the *non-self*."[1] This curiosity about what was not part of his own being and about what he had not himself created helps us to understand his love of foreign travel, which we shall examine in the next chapter. It also made it easy for him, as a lover of literature, to become a critic of the works of other writers.

There was another aspect to his character that had an influence on his becoming a critic. Louise Dillingham pointed out long ago that Gautier was rather timid and that fear was one of his dominant traits.[2] He was not one to sacrifice everything and everybody to his art. He worried about his own financial security and comfort, and he feared for the well-being of those who were dependent on him. He felt the need to provide for his son born in 1836, and by the early 1850's, he was supporting his father and his two sisters, as well as his mistress Ernesta Grisi and two children that she had borne him. Gautier knew that poetry could not pay the rent, and as for prose, *Mademoiselle de Maupin* had earned him only 1500 francs and *Les Jeunes-France* only 400. Journalistic criticism could at least provide him with a regular income and permit him to maintain a middle-class standard of living.

As early as 1831 Gautier had begun to contribute art criticism to obscure and sometimes ephemeral journals. *Ariel, journal du monde élégant*, for instance, lasted only long enough for several issues to appear, but these did include articles by Gautier on paintings exhibited in annual *salons*. *Ariel's* eagerness to accept his offerings can no doubt be explained by the fact that Gautier himself, in collaboration with Charles Lasailly, had founded it, but there were other magazines more than willing to accept his efforts, like *La France littéraire* and *Le Cabinet de lecture*. These modest beginnings provided Gautier with the experience needed for his career as a professional critic, which began in 1836 when he was hired by Emile de Girardin as art and theater columnist for *La Presse*. At first he received some fifty francs per article, but by 1845 or 1846, with his increasing reputation as a man of letters, his wages had reached three times that amount. His contract with Girardin was not an exclusive one, however, for between 1836 and 1838 he also contributed some seventy articles to *Le Figaro*. Despite the volume of his writing in this field, Gautier claimed that he never enjoyed his journalistic writing. His well-known poem "Après le feuilleton" ("After the Column") speaks eloquently of his obligation to go to the theater each week to see some wretched comedy and then waste time reviewing which he would have preferred to spend writing poetry. Actually, Gautier earned a good deal of money working for Girardin, but their relationship was always strained. Gautier was often negligent about turning in material by the necessary deadline, and he chafed at working for a man whose only values were commercial. Finally in 1855 Théophile left *La Presse* to work for the official newspaper of the Second Empire, *Le Moniteur universel*, where he earned perhaps 20,000 francs a year.

The art and theater criticism which constituted the bulk of Gautier's output was what we may call journalistic or public criticism, that is, like a modern newspaper theater or book reviewer, he wrote both to inform the public and to influence its choices. In addition to these topical weekly columns for *La Presse* and other organs, Gautier took pleasure in writing criticism of a more reflective nature, criticism which had no immediate commercial function but simply appealed to his own taste and interests. *Les Grotesques* was an attempt at "literary exhumations" of minor writers of the early seventeenth century. Later in life he wrote lengthy articles, actually monographs, on such giants as Gérard de Nerval, Balzac, and Baudelaire. While his friendship with these men may explain his interest in part, there can be no doubt that he admired them greatly as writers, a judgment that history has ratified. In his later years Gautier composed a long article entitled "Les Progrès de la poésie française depuis 1830," which can still be read today with profit. Finally, he began his *Histoire du romantisme*, which was never finished because he died. All this reflective criticism shows Gautier's deep and enduring love for the history of his nation's literature and testifies to the breadth of his interests.

Like many writers of his day, Gautier became concerned with esthetic theory. In the years preceding and following 1830, the debate swirled constantly about one central point: was there an immutable, eternal beauty, with laws and characteristics that all could come to understand if properly taught, as neoclassicists believed, or was beauty an individual matter, somehow to be equated with the intensity of each artist's passion? Like his contemporaries, Gautier discussed these matters in the *cénacles* and at the cafés, and he sometimes directly, sometimes only implicitly, came to grips with them in his critical articles.

To conclude: Théophile Gautier spanned the entire range of criticism. He dabbled in esthetics, he was a popular critic of art and the theater, and he also wrote monographs on some of the leading writers of his day. The total volume of his criticism is impressively large. In a general book of limited size, however, we shall be obliged to eliminate all but the essentials as we deal in turn with each facet of his critical vision.

I *Gautier's Basic Esthetics*

Art, classicism always proclaimed, held the mirror up to nature, and the artist, while genuine talent was indispensable, was to a considerable extent a craftsman whose goal was to mirror some exterior reality or truth. The doctrine of *imitation* was, then, essential to the classical esthetic, and when theoreticians of this school used the word *imagination*, they tended to mean the poet's capacity to create a picture (image) of an entity existing outside and independent of the artist. But starting in the eighteenth century, especially with Denis Diderot, the meaning of *imagination* changed little by little until it came to refer, especially among the Romantics, to a creative, not a reflective power — a lamp, in Meyer Abrams phrase, not a mirror.[3]

In his book, *The Art Criticism of Théophile Gautier*, M. C. Spencer has done an able job of summarizing the manner in which Gautier developed an esthetic based on each artist's creative imagination, and we cannot do better than to follow his exposition.[4] In *Mademoiselle de Maupin*, Albert may frequently talk the language of immutable beauty, but he has more modern ideas as well. "All men," he remarks, "have within themselves all of humanity, and by writing whatever comes into his mind, [the writer] succeeds better than if he copies with a magnifying glass objects placed outside himself" (p. 237). A few years later, in his *salon* of 1839, Gautier developed the idea in greater detail. "Goethe said somewhere that all artists carry within themselves a *microcosm,* that is, a complete little world, from which they draw the thought and form of their works; — it is in this microcosm that the blonde heroines and dark-haired madonnas dwell."[5] Artists who draw from their microcosm are not mere imitators but true creators, "poets" in the Greek sense. Delacroix is a prime example of such an artist, Gautier believes, for one can see at a glance that his art is inspired by his inner vision *(vue intérieure)* and as a result has an inevitable harmony and unity.

In 1841 Gautier repeated and amplified this idea. Obviously, even with an "inner vision," representational art of any kind has some starting point "outside" the artist. But more is involved than imitation. For Gautier,

> An Artist is impressed by surrounding nature according to his faculties. The sky leaves in his eyes favorite or particular hues. Certain faces strike him more strongly; he seizes relationships that are invisible to others. But not everyone has the genius or memory to coordinate his impressions and give them logic. Such people fail to create unity because they lack intuition and are distracted by any chance, extraneous detail, by any form that has not been accounted for by official academies or models. M. Delacroix has to the highest degree this gift of assimilating objects, of giving them the colors of his own prism, taking just what is suitable to his idea. . . . When M. Delacroix paints a picture, he looks within himself rather than looking out the window.[6]

While this kind of thinking was in the air, so to speak, during these decades, some scholars believe Gautier's contribution important enough to have had some impact on the development of Baudelaire's esthetics. As early as the *Salon de 1846* we find the author of *Les Fleurs du mal* expressing an esthetic of relativism based on each artist's vision: "Each individual is his [own] harmony," and "Each individual has his own ideal. . . . There are in painters' souls as many ideals as there are individuals, because a portrait is a model complicated by an artist."[7] Because of the individual nature of each artist or writer, a critic should not "champion line over color or color over line," for he cannot know "the proportions of taste for color and line in each artist, nor how these elements become fused in his work. . . . Hence a wider point of view [is needed, which is] individualism." The critic "should command the artist . . . to express his own temperament sincerely, aided by all the techniques his craft can provide."[8]

If Baudelaire was well on his way toward developing a coherent esthetic, one that made him a leading theoretician of the nineteenth century, Gautier was less successful in his art criticism, for he rarely used his microcosm theory except when talking about Delacroix, and in fact, this relativism tended to come into conflict with a more classical view of art. We remember that soon after the premiere of *Hernani* Gautier was making fun of Romanticism's medieval excesses in "Elias Wildmanstadius." Then a little later, in the preface to *Mademoiselle de Maupin,* he cried out in tones that were only partly humorous: "Who will deliver us from the Middle Ages?" Finally, looking back over his life more than thirty years later, he concluded: "I liked cathedrals very much because of Notre-Dame de Paris, but the sight of the Parthenon cured me of the Gothic malady, which never was a very serious disease with me."[9] The fact is that despite Gautier's Romanticism, the universality of the classical ideal had never ceased to appeal to him.

Gautier's classical esthetic needs to be understood quite precisely. While theoreticians ever since Horace had worried about the ethical side of classical art and had preached that the purpose of art was to delight and instruct, Gautier had no patience with artistic expression that dealt with good. During the 1830's "the good" was being defined as social progress, and Gautier made it clear that he was not interested in such nonsense. He once insisted that he would cheerfully give up his French citizenship for a painting by Raphaël or for a beautiful naked woman.[10] His concern was uniquely with the beautiful.

But the beautiful was never in Gautier's eyes an aspect of that sterile classicism of the eighteenth century, with its facile doctrines of imitation that led to such extremes as the *trompe l'oeil* effect. His ideal was rather the painter Ingres, a Classicist, Gautier felt, of a more profound kind. Writing a laudatory article on that painter for *L'Artiste* in 1857, Gautier almost seemed to make him a Romantic. He spoke of his energy as a painter and of Ingres' desire not to paint until inspired. He added: "Ingres, although he may seem classical to the superficial observer, really isn't at all. He goes back directly to ancient sources, to nature, to Greek antiquity."[11] He went on to explain that Ingres had no use for academic stuffiness and that when he painted an ancient subject, he preferred to turn for inspiration to Aeschylus, Euripides, and Sophocles rather than to modern "Classicists" like Racine and his imitators. Gautier had this same love for Ancient Greece. During his trip to Athens in 1852, he almost literally prayed before the "perfect, absolute, and true beauty" of the Parthenon.[12] In contemplation "before this work which is so pure, so noble, so beautiful, so totally in harmony with divine rhythm," he was indeed a Classicist in the best and most profound sense of the word. If Gautier hesitated to call Ingres classical, it was but an apparent confusion of language. Gautier was trying to distinguish between ancient classical and what he considered the less desirable French classical of the seventeenth and eighteenth centuries. Gautier had little interest in the "rigorous and mathematical symmetry" of the neoclassicists and preferred a more subtle balancing of groups.

In 1847 Gautier tried to reconcile the two opposing polarities of his esthetics. In an article dealing with the Swiss artist, Rodolphe Töpffer, he retained the idea of a *petit monde* (or microcosm) inside the artist which serves as a focal point for transmuting reality into art. But in a departure from the microcosm articles of 1839 and 1841, which — as Spencer shrewdly noted — had not even mentioned the word beauty, Gautier now stressed that while "an artist is above all a man, and can reflect in his work . . . loves, hates, passions, beliefs, and prejudices of his day, it is with the understanding that art, which is sacred, will always be for him the goal and not the means. Anything done for any reason other than to satisfy the eternal rules of the beautiful can have no value for the future."[13] As he had done in the preface to *Mademoiselle de Maupin*, he once again preached that modern artists should "seek beauty for itself with complete impartiality and with perfect disinterestedness, without predicating success on allusions or tendencies foreign to the subject being treated."[14]

Any phraseology that refers to "seeking beauty for itself" is directly within the tradition of the doctrine of Art for Art's sake.[15] Gautier had already embraced this concept in the preface to *Maupin*, but since 1835 the doctrine had come under attack from all sides. Traditional Classicists wanted a work to instruct as well as to please, and as we said earlier, the Romantics were turning increasingly to utilitarian concepts of social progress. Critics of Gautier tended in their attacks to separate form and content and then accuse him and others of advocating "form for form's sake." Gautier defended himself vigorously: "The great error of the adversaries of the doctrine of art for art's sake . . . is to believe that form can be independent of the idea; the form cannot be produced without the idea nor the idea without the form. . . . Art for Art's sake does not mean form for form's sake, but form for beauty's sake, with all irrelevant meanings, all doctrines, and all direct utility removed."[16]

Gautier's esthetics, then, do not culminate in any orthodox Classical doctrine, for as we noted above, he rejected the concept of "good" or of elevating man's being through the "instructive" side of art. Nor, as he abandoned — at least in part — his concept of the microcosm, can he be said to belong to the individualistic tradition of Romanticism. Rather than reconciling his two polarities, he created a kind of unity for his criticism that went beyond them and espoused a third viewpoint based on an uncompromising idealism. As early as the preface to *Maupin* he had denigrated art based on utility or reality, grumbling that the most useful place in the house was the toilet.[17] He was completely unable to accept or appreciate the realism of Gustave Courbet and in later years that of Manet. Yet even on the matter of realism it is unwise to assume that Gautier's position is a simple one. Gautier recognized that the great Spanish painters Murillo, Velasquez, Ribera, and Goya used reality — and often a very grim reality — as a point of departure for their painting, yet he always admired them greatly.

As we look back over more than a century, what seems at first glance to be the most important aspect of Gautier's esthetics is this championing of art for art's sake, or as he might have put it, art for beauty's sake. To him, beauty was the plastic form and the idealized line, and much of his descriptive technique is an effort to transpose perfect form into words. Indeed, more than with any other writer of nineteenth-century France, we associate today this doctrine with Théophile Gautier's name. But perhaps Gautier's most vital contribution lay elsewhere. Even if he failed to develop the idea fully and if it was not altogether original with him, he made a modest contribution to the development and propagation of an esthetic of relativism through the theory of the microcosm. Twentieth-century esthetics is the direct offspring of this earlier understanding.

II *Gautier's Practical Art Criticism*

If Gautier rarely used the microcosm theory in his everyday practice of art criticism, it was because he believed in it only partly, and also because the critic needed to be familiar with the artist's temperament as well as with a good number of his works in order for it to work well. This was possible in the case of Delacroix, whom Gautier knew personally and whose greatness made his canvases well known, but the *salon* system of exhibiting paintings normally made this method hard to apply. The majority of artists, as is always the case, were but little known, and their paintings were usually hung at random.

Since a personal approach to criticism was not readily feasible, one might suppose that Gautier, a painter himself who had spent months in an artist's studio, would have wanted to display his technical knowledge of color, composition, and line as aspects of a kind of classical criticism. But Gautier rarely did this either, at least not in any systematic way. Gautier's practical criticism was of an entirely different order. It was strongly influenced by Diderot's idea that the critic should describe in words the painting that he is looking at so that a reader can "see" the canvas and can experience, insofar as possible, the same emotions as would a viewer. This idea was reinforced among members of the generation of 1830 by the theory of the transposition of art, that is, the belief that one can express one art medium in terms of another. Behind this theory lies the fundamental concept (that Baudelaire would develop further) of a vast system of correspondences partly visible behind ordinary phenomena.

Whatever the reason for Gautier's interest, he was captivated by art transpositions and during the rest of his life often tried to "redo" paintings into poems or set pieces of prose description. The result of this technique was in practice to equate description and analysis. Most of the time he would describe a painting — enthusiastically, if possible, for like Diderot he believed in praise — with a few general comments on light, color, or line, and then pronounce his verdict. His penchant for description, already visible in his criticism of the 1830's, became even more pronounced as the years passed. The following example, taken from the *Moniteur universel* of December 14, 1867, will serve as a typical example. Writing of Théodore Rousseau's *Allée des châtaigniers* ("Chestnut Tree Walk), Gautier exclaimed:

> What power, what strength, what lushness! The walkway plunges into shade flecked with sunlight, like a cathedral of nature, to use the style popular at the time of Chateaubriand, and which was as good as any other, between two rows of tree trunks, like groups of Gothic pillars, mixing like fillets on a vault their gigantic branches with their knotty joints, with their

large spatula-like leaves. How the sap races under the rugged bark, in these thick branches with their deep coolness! How the secret life of vegetation flows through these masses of greenery and the thick grasses. . . . In this unrivaled work, Théodore Rousseau, while maintaining an unquestioned originality, recalls to some extent Hobbema's robustness, and that powerful master whom the English call familiarly "Old Crane." Never was nature more intimately studied and more broadly rendered, with such intensity of effect, and with such profound and true poetry.[18]

Gautier has tried to make us "see" the painting, to sense its dramatic composition, while at the same time making sure that the reader recognizes the critic's wide literary and artistic knowledge. This impressionistic treatment appealed widely to the public of Gautier's day. It may even have had, as some claim, an influence on the art criticism of Edmond and Jules de Goncourt, major art critics of the nineteenth century. But if Gautier's public appreciated this kind of criticism, today we are much less impressed, and our interest in his later art criticism is reduced even more by the fact that Gautier did not always bother to see the canvases himself. He would send a substitute who took notes which would serve as a basis for Gautier's commentary. Except when Gautier describes a canvas that has been lost, his criticism has little of enduring value. Spencer's judgment is harsh, but fair: "Only a small portion of Gautier's work as an art critic deserves to survive."[19]

III *Gautier the Theater Critic*

For more than twenty-five years, Gautier wrote a weekly column of theatrical criticism, except during the summer when theaters were closed and when he was traveling abroad. At times Nerval, who also wrote for *La Presse,* would do his column for him. Despite Gautier's occasional respite from this weekly chore, the volume of his theatrical criticism is impressive. When Hetzel published the majority of it under the title, *Histoire de l'art dramatique en France depuis vingt-cinq ans* (1858 - 59), it comprised six volumes, each with 350 pages of small print.[20]

The fact that Gautier wrote so much theater criticism led him to consider the nature of plays and the criteria by which they should be judged. As late as 1851, we find Gautier still under the influence of Hugo's preface to *Cromwell,* when he wrote: "Theater is the last art form [of a society]. It comes along after the ode and the epic. It can make both a dream and a story seem real, it puts before your eyes what the imagination alone could conceive. . . . The lyric poet speaks in his own name and reads his soul; the epic poet tells of the deeds of his hero; the dramatic poet cannot have their freshness of invention. He takes his subject from legends and popular stories. . . . Shakespeare pilfered right and left . . . [and] Corneille borrowed from the Spaniards."[21]

The idea that the theater is the last literary form of a culture is of course nonsense, as would have been obvious to Gautier had he stopped to consider the fact that the lyric poetry of his day came well after an established theatrical tradition. And there can be no doubt that Gautier, unlike many Frenchmen of that era, knew France's theatrical tradition from its very beginnings. In a later chapter we shall see the influence of medieval theater and the *commedia dell'arte* on his own attempts at writing plays. But with a few exceptions, Gautier's public theater criticism considers the theatrical tradition only since the seventeenth century. This limitation in scope was no doubt due to the fact that, as we remarked in our opening chapter, pseudo-Racinian dramas were still being written for the Parisian stage.

While Gautier shared the dissatisfaction of the young Romantics with these neoclassical survivals, he was in fact so imbued with his own culture that he could not conceive of tragedy outside the Racinian tradition. He defined tragedy as a "poem in dialogue, of epic style, where the misfortunes of kings and nobles and heroes unfold . . . in the same room of the palace within twenty-four hours" (May 27, 1844). No wonder neither he nor Hugo could think of Shakespeare's plays, with their mixture of the noble and the ignoble, as being "tragedies." So disgusted were the Romantics with the "rhymed boredom" (May 27, 1844) of their own theater, that they abandoned the word tragedy itself, preferring to use the word *drame* to distinguish "compositions where one finds terrifying situations and burlesque ones, or at least familiar ones, intermingled" (July 8, 1844), again an echo of Hugo's preface to *Cromwell.*

Gautier's instincts were sound. French theater had indeed needed changing, and the Romantics were the innovators. Gautier suggested that the normal five acts could perhaps be reduced to three. He argued that a play needs an exposition, a complication, and a dénouement. With five acts, there are always two, the second and the fifth, which cause trouble, the former repeating the first act, and the latter an unnecessary appendage to the fourth. Furthermore, having abandoned the idea that tragedy is an inherently superior genre, he was willing to accept comedy as the equal of tragedy or the *drame*. After seeing innumerable plays, Gautier concluded that they "have all been alike since the world was formed, [since] the human spirit has been able to invent only two types, one where you get killed, and the other where you get married" (April 26, 1847), in other words, tragedy and comedy. As for the latter, he would have preferred to see more comedies of manners, which satirized social types incisively in the manner of Molière and Lesage, but between governmental censorship and the growth of the novel, which was replacing the theater as a vehicle for social commentary, there was little satirical vigor on the stage (e.g., September 22, 1845).

Taking an even larger view, Gautier mused on the nature of the theatrical effect itself. Already in *Mademoiselle de Maupin* he had preached in favor of a theater of fantasy.[22] He saw it as a form of the ideal, which we remember was his goal in art. Expanding on this idea, he wrote on July 31, 1837: "In general what modern theater lacks is ideality and poetry. Prosaism is invading everything, there is no longer any place anywhere for fantasy." He tried to give intellectual substance to his feelings that a realistic theater was undesirable: "In the theater, we agree with the Chinese on painting. They like only bizarre and chimerical creations: a painter who copies nature as it is seems to them a man of little talent and imagination. Real life is not so joyous that its facsimile should be put on the stage" (March 19, 1841). His conclusion is a logical outgrowth of such ideas: "Art cannot exist without conventions; the absence of conventions will bring about the ruination of the theater. The stage demands a point of view that is not well understood today. . . . A drama cannot be true, it must have some parts [of reality] sacrificed, others exaggerated" (July 31, 1837). No wonder Gautier enjoyed Musset's theater, even if it was written largely in prose, for Musset was the most whimsical of all the nineteenth-century French dramatists. Gautier also enjoyed the *féerie à grand spectacle*, a special kind of production of fairy tales or legends with ingenious and beautiful costumes and décor. Gautier's interest in a theater of convention and fantasy even led him to appreciate the lowly farce. "Farce," he commented, "is a genre as literary as any other; Molière is half farce" (December 20, 1842).

Gautier's weekly fare consisted for the most part of plays with a comic structure — that is, whatever their form, they had a happy ending. The straight comedies were usually bourgeois in tone and setting. The vaudevilles, which had been martial and patriotic under Napoleon, had by mid-century become as middle-class as the comedies, thanks to the efforts of playwrights like Eugène Scribe. The only difference was that, as in a modern musical comedy, someone would periodically burst into song. The melodramas were a bit different. The action was transferred from the bourgeois *salon* to some more exotic setting like a Gothic castle or a bandit's lair, and they had greater intensity (or, when badly done, greater absurdity). Otherwise all these plays were very similar. They all had a hero, a heroine, and a villain.

Curiously, Gautier came to enjoy good melodrama. He knew the fiction of Ann Radcliffe, which had made the Gothic novel popular, and was familiar with the earlier melodramas of Guilbert de Pixérécourt. Writing of *Les Ruines de Vaudemont,* he remarked only half-jokingly that "as soon as you hear the title, you are seized with terror, and you shiver just looking at the posters announcing the play" (March 3, 1845). His mockery cannot hide the fact that he was like most of us. Deep within us lies something powerfully attracted to this "discredited" genre. But since intellectual factors are normally dominant in criticism, and on that plane it is obvious that melodramas are absurd, Gautier quickly learned to make fun of the inevitable formulas of melodrama and indeed of all standard comedy: "When you have a daughter, you want to marry her off, and naturally to someone she doesn't love. That's what fathers are for. . . . Without them, all plays would end after Scene 1, there would be a marriage and that would be that" (October 23, 1843). When a villain appears, Gautier notes appreciatively that the scoundrel, in this case a pirate, "is dressed in black from head to foot, and is equally black inside. He is one of those fine types out of old-style melodrama which do not tolerate any shading of characterization" (August 21, 1837), and he was amused enough to accept the exaggerated manner in which the actors rolled their r's and hissed their s's. When a hero is shot in Act II, Gautier is unruffled: "Don't worry . . . the hero of a play cannot die in Act II" (July 20, 1841). Gautier knew not only hero and villain but all the stock devices of this theater. When he saw a blonde girl among gypsies, he commented joyfully: "Everybody knows that gypsies are great kidnapers — especially on the stage — and one doesn't have to be very clever, honey, to guess that you have tucked in your bodice a locket or a cross, which will permit you to be recognized by your true parents" (April 6, 1846). Eventually, Gautier got to the point where, he said, he could guess the plot after the opening two or three sentences.

Faced with the stereotyped characters and the conventional plots of most of the plays he reviewed, Gautier, already conditioned by the practice of his art criticism, fell back on lengthy summary. Indeed, the very reason for the publication of his six volumes of reviews was, in the editor's words, "[his] talent for descriptions which has made him universally recognized as one of the most knowledged masters in the art of writing. With what humorous verve, and with what brilliant, colorful, picturesque language, he knows how to write up a play."[23] These descriptive pieces were not only of value in letting the public know whether to stay home or not, they often made good reading and were in many cases more interesting than the plays themselves.

A serious artist himself, Gautier knew that ninety per cent of the plays he saw were worthless, but to have said so in his column was not possible. He had to assume the standards of the potential audience, at least in part. He tried to make a virtue of necessity: "Criticism," he remarked, "is not, as people imagine, the hunting out of weaknesses, it is the search for beauty" (December 16, 1844), and he preferred to praise if he could, because "admiring is such a sweet thing to do" (July 1, 1844). In the preface to *Mademoiselle de Maupin* Gautier had compared critics to eunuchs, unable to create, only able to watch the master's (i.e., the artist's) sport. Now his view was different. Critics are not "bilious, livid beings who eat gall and drink absinthe" (February 8, 1843), he asserted, explaining that he knew full well that hostile criticism could be corrosive, inflicting serious wounds on an artist. "How many times, at the risk of appearing negligent or out of touch with things, have we kept silent, when we had nothing [favorable] to say" (February 23, 1846). But whenever he thought about the manner in which the modern press exploited his talents, he was less charitable. "Criticism," he grumbled, "is only free advertising" (February 8, 1843).

There was one level at which ordinary comedy and melodrama could become serious. With any comedy (just as with romances in prose fiction), the hero represents "good" ideas, the villain "bad" ones, and the heroine, won by the hero, represents the reward for being right. As the plots of comedy tend to have a basic similarity, comedy and romance vary their eternal monotony by espousing social causes of the moment. As long as the villain incarnates such vices as avarice or lechery in opposition to the hero's generosity or chastity, one might even be under the illusion that there are no ideas at all in this theater, but when political positions are attached to hero and villain, the ideological structures of comedy and melodrama become visible — and controversial. Gautier quickly noted this tendency when he first became a regular critic: "Society has been preached at all summer by the vaudevilles. . . . They have preached in turn the value of saving or of serving in the National Guard, and so forth" (September 4, 1837). This was all rather harmless, but even so, Gautier did not care for it: "Vaudeville must not go beyond its mission and pose as a preacher" (March 21, 1838), he said, unaware that it is the very nature of a comedy to preach *something*.

When in 1839 Gautier reviewed a play with a political message, he protested even more strongly, for this drama of revolt during the Middle Ages assumed the virtue of the downtrodden. "The lower classes," Gautier grumbled, "have been flattered long enough. Under a rough exterior, the serfs, or if you prefer, the proletariat, hide just as deep corruption as the lords with their shapely legs and white hands, and this prejudice of putting all the virtue on one side and vice on the other strikes us as supremely false" (March 25, 1839). After the Revolution of 1848, Gautier felt he must hide his innate conservatism for fear of losing his job. Now he readily agreed that the nobility of the *ancien régime* had been selfish and shortsighted: "In their eyes, the bourgeois were like May flies, vague forms that appeared for a moment between the past and the future, but whom no one remembered, whereas the nobles, eternal thanks to their genealogies, seemed to consider each family a powerful entity coexisting with the ages" (November 6, 1848). Falling in step with the new republicanism, he applauded the idea of making cheap seats available at the Théâtre Français (which had just been renamed the Théâtre de la République) for the honest artisan and his family. He explained: "We must give to the masses the feeling for art, without which nations are but multitudes carried by the dark waters into the abyss of oblivion. Beauty has enormous moral power, its charm touches people who would not be reached by morality alone." If this comment may have been sincere, his next remark could not be: "The great collective soul which hovers over the assemblies of sincere men comes into contact with a divine element, the celestial part of the universe" (March 28, 1848). Gautier's elitish nature could never have approved such democratic mysticism.

On the whole, then, Gautier was repelled by politico-social commentary on the stage. When reviewing a didactic play a year after revolutionary ardor had somewhat cooled, he was unhappy, even when the play in question preached a reactionary message with which he might well have agreed: "The politico-satirical rhapsodies are profoundly disgusting. We could have excused such vaudevilles during the first months of the Republic, because courage excuses everything, and to preach an opinion . . . when there is danger in doing so, is always honorable, but now such postures [are] without risk" (March 5, 1849). He was delighted when reviewing Autran's *La Fille d'Eschyle* to note "this pure literary success at a time when politics seems to absorb everyone" (March 27, 1848). Gautier's desire to avoid political confrontation was a reflection of his own temperament which shied away from involvement. It also reflected his tendency to get along with any regime in power. In this respect he was not unlike Flaubert, who saw folly in all social constructs. Gautier, when it came to comedy, preferred to see "good" and "bad" ideas remain generalized and nonpolitical.

Gautier's theatrical criticism has often been considered of little value, sometimes because we cannot be sure whether he wrote a given column, partly because he summarized to such a great extent, and summary is not criticism. Politically inspired critics object to his conservatism and even more to his tendency to bend with the political breeze. But reading his criticism is a pleasant experience. He shows flashes of insight into theatrical problems; he accepts and takes interest in — perhaps because he must — genres that have all too often been neglected; and above all, he did have the ability to write charming and witty résumés of the plays he saw. The criticism is not great, but it would be a pity if it were to be totally forgotten.

IV *Gautier's Reflective Literary Criticism*

At the beginning of this chapter we referred to Gautier's "reflective" criticism, that is, literary analyses free from the immediate commercial pressure of his art and theater columns. This writing was inspired by his reflecting at leisure upon French literature, past and present, which he deeply loved. In fact, it was with some essays on unknown or unpopular writers of the past, especially of the early seventeenth century, that Gautier began his career.[24]

It should not be assumed, however, that these essays are all attempts at rehabilitation. Such authors as Scalion de Virbluneau, Pierre de Saint-Louis, and Guillaume Colletet were simply dreadful writers judged by any standard, and Gautier's pleasure is derived from their very ineptness, which he describes in a half-critical, half-delighted tone. But there is more to *Les Grotesques* (the title he gave to these essays) than this kind of facile enjoyment, as his study of Chapelain makes clear. Jean Chapelain (1595 - 1674) is known today as a literary critic. It was he who wrote the censure of Corneille's *Le Cid* for the new Académie Française and conceived the idea for the Academy's dictionary. In general, he was a strong believer in classical literary forms and as a theoretician was influential during the second third of the seventeenth century. But his own epic poem, *La Pucelle* ("The Maid of Orleans"), of which twelve cantos appeared after twenty years of hard work, was a distinct failure. Musing on the phenomenon of a critic turned poet, Gautier wrote: "[Chapelain's] work is very reasonable, well developed, well structured, as they say nowadays, and could have been a true poem had it been written by someone else." Explaining his judgment, Gautier adds: "Chapelain went at it backwards. He learned Greek, Latin, Spanish, Italian, rhetoric, and poetics; he read Aristotle, and carefully meditated on how an epic should be written, whether a woman can be a hero, whether mythological figures are permissible in a Christian poem. . . . He would have done much better . . . to let the critics debate all these problems — for that is their function — and to plow his furrow on Parnassus as hard as he could, worrying only about finishing. A field plowed this way gives beautiful golden ears of wheat among which bloom red poppies and blue cornflowers. Only thistles grow in the thin soil of treatises and prefaces on art" (pp. 269 - 70). Gautier concluded: "The poet is a keyboard and nothing more. Each passing idea puts its finger on a key; — the key gives off its note. That's all there is to it. Nobody thinks a piano is a musician: poets are the pianos of the multitude [la foule]. Some have more octaves than others." Gautier's attack on Chapelain's poetry is in the Romantic tradition, for it is based on the necessity of the poet's being more than a craftsman. Gautier perhaps oversimplifies Classicism a little, partly because in 1830 understanding of it was not as subtle as it is today, and partly for reasons of contemporary polemics, but there can be no doubt that his dissection of Chapelain's epic is basically sound. Gautier was also astute enough to appreciate a poet like Saint-Amand. He enjoyed Saint-Amand's "La Solitude," for he saw in it "nature studied directly and not through the works of former masters. . . . The poet . . . describes what he sees . . . with a freedom and delicacy of touch which reveals a master" (p. 168). Gautier also praised Théophile de Viau, and his lengthy essay on this poet marks perhaps the beginning of the trend that would lead to our twentieth-century realization that he was a major poet. Gautier is modern enough to use the word "baroque" for these writers, and he enjoyed their personal vision of the world. In 1834 he was not yet using the word *microcosm*, but the idea was already implied.

The most important essay in *Les Grotesques* deals with a still earlier writer, the fifteenth-century poet, François Villon. It consists both of lengthy selections from his poetry, presented most admiringly, and of a running commentary on Villon's life as revealed through his work. Gautier found the crudity of Villon's language a refreshing change from the artificiality of many fifteenth-century rhymers and the false naiveté of many medieval ballads. Further, he understood, as many bourgeois did not, that despite his vulgarity, Villon was a highly moral poet in that he knew that debauchery created its own hell.[25] This is why Gautier says that Villon is almost the only medieval poet who really has ideas (p. 5). Gautier also appreciates Villon for giving us a picture of some aspects of life during the late Middle Ages: the taverns, the whores, and the thieves, but he admires even more Villon's art. "A single word, a single touch," he remarks, "are enough for Villon to bring a character alive; he siezes the distinctive trait with sagacity; a name and an epithet, and a man is constructed out of nothing" (p. 36). Nor is Gautier unaware of the formal aspects of Villon's work. He finds parallels between his octosyllabic verse with its *abab* rhymes and those of Byron in *Don Juan*. Above all, Gautier the Romantic is sensitive to the personal element in Villon: "The *I* recurs frequently in his poetry. He speaks of himself, confesses himself with charming naiveté. He comes back to himself, he enjoys recalling the good days of his youth; he discusses death, virtue, everything . . . with digressions and ironical legacies" (p. 13). With the exception of the fact that Gautier, like all earlier critics, was unaware that there is a good deal of literary convention in this very "personal" poet, his essay is an important contribution to the rehabilitation of Villon's reputation.

Gautier's interest in a writer's personal feelings was no doubt one reason why he became interested in his contemporaries, for he could truly get to know them. In the 1850's and 1860's he used this personal knowledge in an official way, writing necrological articles for *Le Moniteur*. More important, he wrote monographs on his friends Gérard de Nerval, Honoré de Balzac, and Charles Baudelaire. These and other shorter essays are primarily biographical, but there does emerge from the total corpus of his writing enough genuine criticism to give us a fair picture of Gautier's understanding (outside the theater) of the literature of his day.

Gautier never believed that prose should be considered the equal of poetry. He frequently commented that a poet can write great prose, but a great prose writer — like Chateaubriand — can never compose decent verse. Furthermore, as we remember that in painting Gautier had little use for the realists, it is not difficult to guess that he would tend not to appreciate the budding realistic school of French writers as well. Indicative of his attitude is the fact that he rarely mentions Stendhal and shows little interest in Flaubert's novels. But realistic fiction was so important after 1830 that even Gautier could not ignore it totally, especially when some of its major practitioners were his personal friends. Gautier had met Edmond and Jules de Goncourt in the offices of *L'Artiste* in 1856, and through them he became acquainted with the lithographer Gavarni. He wrote brief articles on these "Naturalists." At about the same time, in 1858, Gautier wrote a very long essay on Balzac, who was not only his friend but the man who made the social novel the dominant form of fiction in France. Gautier's criticism of these artists merits consideration.

Curiously, when dealing with Gavarni, the Goncourts, and Balzac, Gautier seems to show none of the hostility to Realism that was evident in his comments on Courbet. Musing on the contradictions in his own attitude, he wrote: "The ancient world still dominates us to such a degree that we are barely aware of the civilization around us. . . . Each year, thousands of young Greeks and Romans leave our schools knowing nothing about modern life. — More than anyone else, we have admired the persistent strength of the [Platonic] Idea and the eternal power of the beautiful; but isn't it odd that art reflects our contemporary period so little?"[26] Turning then to Gavarni, Gautier added: "His is the considerable merit of being frankly, exclusively, absolutely modern; like Balzac, with whom he has many parallels, he has done his own Human Comedy."[27] Gavarni is a Realist in that he had "no interest in traditional forms. . . . No one is better acquainted than he with our scrawny bodies emaciated by civilization; he knows about the . . . baldness of the Parisian dandy, [and] the grotesque obesity, the limp wrinkles . . . of the bankers and so-called serious men." He concludes by calling Gavarni a "great anatomist" (p. 333). In like fashion, he praised the Goncourts' efforts in the novel: "They tried to render with implacable detail and clarity the reality which was stretched out on their table like an anatomical subject. Their pen was as sharp as a scalpel" (pp. 199 - 200). One recognizes in this clinical imagery Sainte-Beuve's lament in his essay on Flaubert's *Madame Bovary* that he finds "anatomists and physiologists everywhere."

The remarks on Gavarni and the Goncourts are relatively brief. The bulk of his commentary on Realistic fiction appears in his essay on Balzac. Gautier makes very clear Balzac's contribution to the development of French literature. Discussing what had been the tradition of the *roman* prior to 1830, he wrote:

> Up to then, the *roman* had been but the depiction of a single passion, love, but love in an ideal sphere outside the necessities and miseries of life. . . . The characters . . . neither ate nor drank, nor lived anywhere, nor had a bill at the tailor's. They moved in an abstract milieu as in a [French Classical] tragedy. If they desired to travel, they would leave without a passport and take a few handfuls of diamonds from their pockets and pay the coachmen with them, never failing to drive the horses until they dropped. . . . With a profound instinct for reality Balzac understood that modern life was dominated by one great fact — money — and in *La Peau de chagrin* ["The Wild Ass's Skin"] he had the courage to describe a lover worried not only whether he had touched the heart of the girl he loved, but whether he had enough money to pay for the cab.[28]

Gautier shows clear appreciation of the fact that prose fiction was moving from a romance to a novel-centered view and that Balzac, with all his love for the extravagant, was instrumental in bringing about this change. Gautier understood, too, that Balzac's plan to paint a vast tableau of modern French society was unparalleled in literature. But although Gautier recognized Balzac's gifts as an observer, he sensed that the author of *La Comédie humaine* was no plodding Realist in the manner of Champfleury, the leader in 1857 and 1858 of the Realistic School. He felt the importance of a short story by Balzac called "Facino Cane," in which the author-narrator speaks of his ability to evaluate people he sees in the street not only by means of minute observation of their exterior, but also by an intuitive penetration into the heart of their being. Balzac, Gautier comments, has an "inner eye" which can see all humanity. Then reaching back to his essays on Delacroix for the word, Gautier concludes that Balzac is a complete "microcosm" (p. 112). This is excellent criticism, and modern scholars have really not gone much farther, at least insofar as general principles are concerned. If it must be added that Gautier's perception is not entirely original (Sainte-Beuve in an essay written shortly after Balzac's death in 1850 makes essentially the same points), Gautier's monograph seems more appealing today. Unlike Sainte-Beuve, who grumbled at Balzac's poor style, Gautier coupled his criticism with genuine admiration.

Gautier's main love was of course poetry. He wrote a long article in 1867 — again for *L'Artiste* — on his late friend, the poet Gérard de Nerval. It is a sensitive, charming, and intelligent essay that shows Gautier's deep love for his friend, but one finds little or no sustained literary criticism. Gautier does observe that as a poet Nerval first wrote a kind of tender and sentimental verse in the manner of some eighteenth-century elegiacs and then later developed an incredibly complex system of cosmogonic myths which undergirded his hermetic poetry. Gautier sensed, too, that "each word is a symbol,"[29] but there is no close textual analysis nor any attempt to clarify Nerval's thought.

Gautier's main effort in the field of poetry criticism was his monograph, "Les Progrès de la poésie française depuis 1830" (1868),[30] which was commissioned by the French government. It begins with André Chénier in the late eighteenth century, and after hurrying through the Romantics, tries to assess the many poets flourishing in mid-century. Inevitably we find names like Joseph Soulary or A. Lacaussade, unknown even to specialists today, but for the most part Gautier showed an ability to select poets of real talent, given the fact that his essay was written before it was possible to have any knowledge of Verlaine or Rimbaud. He stressed Baudelaire, although tending to see him as an extreme Romantic of a decadent kind, whose art reflected modern civilization in its complexity and its fatigue. For Gautier, Baudelaire's poetry is "supple, complex, both objective and subjective, exploring, curious, finding words in every dictionary and colors on every palette" (p. 304). Gautier feels the beauty of Baudelaire's darkly inspired verse: "Does not night which brings out a million stars, night with its changing moon and the long, lacy tails of its comets, its northern lights, its mysterious shadows and fear, have its own worth and its own poetry" (p. 305)? Gautier also appreciated the austere genius of Charles Leconte de Lisle and his leadership in the so-called Parnassian School. In this connection, he recognized the importance of the first issue of *Le Parnasse contemporain*, which appeared in 1866. Throughout the monograph, Gautier is not only informed about titles and poetical content, he also succeeds in communicating the special flavor and tone of each writer.

As far as modern poetics are concerned, Gautier starts with the premise that neoclassical verse of the previous century was "false poetry" (p. 257), and that the "new [Romantic] school avoided mythological terminology. It preferred breeze to zephyr, and the sea was the sea and not Neptune" (p. 257). As for rhythms, Gautier mentions on occasion the craft of poetry, "an art that one learns, which has its methods, its formulae, its secrets, its counterpoint and its harmonies" (p. 291), and he sometimes criticizes poets for sloppy composition. We have here another example of a split type of criticism, one in which he praises the semantic revolution of Romanticism and the craftsmanship of the Classicists. But perhaps in part because of limitations of space, Gautier does not go into detail concerning these matters. Nor does he try to explain that modern imagery could be generated by nearly any concrete object which the poet could then invest with his own meaning. Furthermore, writing in 1868, it was just about impossible for him to see that as the century progressed poets were becoming less and less willing to explain the private meanings that they were giving to their images (Gautier no doubt thought Nerval an isolated oddity), with the result that poetry was becoming increasingly hermetic. Not only could Gautier not know Verlaine and Rimbaud, he saw Stéphane Mallarmé only in his earliest Parnassian phase. Gautier's analyses were further limited by his idea, which he had used so extensively in his art criticism, that the critic should make the reader feel the effect of the poem or the painting. As a case in point, he summarizes Leconte de Lisle's poetry as "producing the effect of a Doric temple silhouetting its whiteness against a backdrop of purple mountains or a blue sky" (p. 288). We may also suspect that his many years of journalistic art and theater criticism had so conditioned him that he fell back unconsciously on facile summary or description.

A final comment on this criticism is in order. It might seem that Gautier was limited in his appreciation of poetry to the Romantic and to the Parnassian. But Gautier had a wider vision than one might suppose. As a kind of epilogue to "Les Progrès de la poésie," he brought his audience up to date on Victor Hugo, in exile on the island of Guernsey. Unable to mention Hugo's opposition to Napoleon III, whose government had commissioned his essay, Gautier limited himself to less controversial works like *Les Contemplations* and *La Légende des siècles*. Gautier was in some ways very different from Hugo, yet he not only recognized the grandiose scope of Hugo's later poetry, he admired it greatly, and he expressed his admiration in terms worthy of Hugo himself or of any good modern critic: "One might say that it was written on Patmos, with an eagle for a writing desk and in the swirl of prophetic hallucinations. Never have the inexpressible and that which has hitherto never been thought been reduced to the formulae of articulated language. . . . It seems that the poet, in this region where there is no longer either contour or color, shadow or light, time or finitude, has heard and taken note of the mysterious whispering of the infinite" (p. 342). In the nineteenth century few critics had the breadth of vision to assess at their true worth poets as different as Hugo, Baudelaire, and Leconte de Lisle.

Théophile Gautier made a modest contribution to literary esthetics and wrote some "reflective" criticism of high quality, but the bulk of his criticism was journalistic. If he was not a radical innovator in this sphere, it must be remembered that a man too far ahead of his time is usually ignored, and no weekly columnist can survive indifference. Gautier was appreciated during his day, and for good reason. He was extremely well read, he had excellent taste in art and literature, and he wrote charmingly. If he often confused summary or biography with criticism, this "flaw" is almost inevitable in popular criticism, and it should not obscure the fact that Gautier raised the level of journalistic criticism of his day to a very high plane.

CHAPTER 4

From La Comédie de la mort *to* Voyage en Espagne

DEATH, like love, has been one of the most obsessive themes in literature. Authors have used it as a device for testing or revealing character, and it has provided the normal ending for tragedy. In the Western world it has taken on a special function because of the dominance of Christian thought. Under the Church's teaching death became for man a moment of solemn judgment, for man's life is weighed at death in the scales of justice. In legend and epic saints, martyrs, and heroes embraced death eagerly, because it offered them an eternity of bliss. In melodrama and romance the villain desperately fought to avoid death, for he knew that the fires of Hell lay beyond the grave. Nor was it wise to try to forget about what lay ahead of each man, Christianity warned. Albrecht Dürer's woodcuts were a grim reminder that man might forget for a time the inevitability of death, but death would certainly not forget him.

With the weakening of the power of the Church, the judgmental aspects of death lost some of their terrors, and during the eighteenth-century Enlightenment many philosophers tried to reduce death to a simple physiological fact. But fear of death seems a staple of man's character, and a clinical, detached attitude has been the exception rather than the rule. The Romantics, at least, showed no such studied indifference. In fact at times they felt a particularly heightened sense of despair before the finality of death, for its presence was a cruel reminder that they were not gods after all, as they tended to feel, but merely mortal men.

But if the Romantics had a more than normal fear of death at times, they had also a corresponding greater hope that death might be a means of access to that better world where the destructive power of time was not a constant threat and where they might live the godlike dream they dreamed. Some of them like Chateaubriand, Lamartine, and Hugo found solace in some form of religious belief.

Alfred de Vigny, on the other hand, faced the end without transcendent faith. But whether believers or not, they all had to face the fact of death squarely and come to terms with it if they were to have any hope of integrating their life and their art.

Théophile Gautier was no exception. There is some evidence to show that in the 1830's, at least, Gautier feared death intensely. We know that he was very superstitious, and superstition is a common indication of the fear of death. Although it is risky to assume that literature reveals life directly, because it is difficult to distinguish between literary convention and personal anguish, most critics have claimed — probably correctly — that Gautier's poems and stories of the 1830's reveal his intensely morbid state of mind.[1] The fear of death appears in Gautier's earliest poetry but even more in some of his stories of the fantastic. We shall reserve the formal study of his exotic and fantastic tales for a later chapter and limit ourselves here to a brief glance at one scene in "Onuphrius," one of the stories of *Les Jeunes-France.*

In a strange nightmare Onuphrius sees himself perfectly lucid but unable to move or to make a sound, surrounded by his friends, given last rites, and buried. To pass the time underground, he begins to compose poetry that describes his own situation. He entitles his verse "Life in Death." This idea and even this very title were to lead to *La Comédie de la mort,* which we may best translate as "The Drama of Death," for there is nothing comic about it.

I La Comédie de la mort

First announced in 1835, *La Comédie de la mort* finally appeared in 1838, published by Desessart. The poems that comprise the section entitled "the drama of death" are only three in number, but they form a sort of prologue of over forty pages to the remaining shorter poems (fifty-six in number) that follow. The opening poem of the prologue, "Portail" ("Portal"), sets the theme of death squarely. Gautier chooses as his principal metaphor the Gothic cathedral whose beautiful, soaring pinnacles have a lugubrious counterpart in the humid mortuary crypts beneath the edifice. The poet then makes a comparison with his own work:

> Mes vers sont les tombeaux tout brodés de sculptures;
> Ils cachent un cadavre, et sous leurs fioritures,
> Ils pleurent bien souvent en paraissant chanter.

(My poems are tombstones covered with sculptures;/They hide a corpse, and under their elaborate forms/They weep frequently when they appear to sing.)

Up to this point, it must be said, the basic idea is within the mainstream of Romanticism, which usually saw death as a threat to the fragile happiness of life on earth. Nor is Gautier any more original when he compares his ambitions and dreams to ships that have set out to sea only to founder and be lost forever. When he calls them "Columbuses unable to find their Americas," we realize that once again he is seeking his paradise lost. But finally the poet shakes off his feeling of hopelessness and seriously tries to discover some means by which he may actually reach his desired goal, and at this juncture he comes up with an idea that was new to him. Rather than sailing directly toward the luminous ideal, he takes another direction. He realizes that his poetry must first go down into the darkness before soaring up into the heavens. Reverting to the image of the cathedral, he exclaims:

En funèbres caveaux creusez-vous, ô mes vers!
Puis montez hardiment comme les cathédrales,
Allongez-vous en tours, tordez-vous en spirales.

(O my poetry, dig down into the mortuary crypts,/Then rise boldly like the cathedrals,/Become soaring towers, twist upward into spirals.)

Gautier was apparently beginning to understand that any heroic quest must involve the facing of reality and death. To descend into hell to confront the monsters and terrors of darkness, however, is a dangerous undertaking. Perhaps Gautier remembered Victor Hugo's warning of the risks of going down into the unknown:

La spirale est profonde, et quand on y descend,
Sans cesse se prolonge et va s'élargissant,
Et pour avoir touché quelque énigme fatale,
De ce voyage obscur souvent on revient pâle.[2]

(The spiral goes deep, and when you go down/It goes on forever and gets wider and wider./And because one has touched some mystery of fate,/One often comes back pale from this dark voyage.)

But the heroic spirit does not hesitate to accept the risks, for he knows that any flight from reality and death marks the false hero and leads to self-destruction. This truth is recognized not only in mythic literature generally but also on the psychological level by modern psychiatry.

The second of the three poems, "La Vie dans la mort" ("Life in

Death"), would lead one to suppose from its title that it develops the idea announced in "Portail," that is, that life comes from descending into death. But the poem is disappointing. It should be noted that part of it was written as early as 1832, which may help to explain why it does not seem to mesh well with "Portail." Moreover, it takes the idea of "life in death" too literally. As was the case with "Onuphrius," this poem deals with sentient corpses in their coffins. Once again the poet imagines a person dead and buried, desperate because he is now forgotten by the world. His mistress is now in another's arms, and his ultimate horror is that he is still conscious, for now death is no longer the "supreme remedy," our last refuge against the ills of this world. In another scene the poet imagines that he can hear a conversation between an earthworm and a dead bride. The woman can feel the worm invading and taking possession of her body. Gautier clearly enjoys describing the macabre eroticism of the scene. He then tries to develop his idea that life comes from death. The worm says:

Console-toi. La Mort donne la vie. — Eclose
A l'ombre d'une croix, l'églantine est plus rose
Et le gazon plus vert.
La racine des fleurs plongera sous tes côtes;
A la place où tu dors les herbes seront hautes;
Aux mains de Dieu tout sert!

(Be consoled. Death gives life. — Blooming/In the shadow of a cross, the wild rose is pinker/And the lawn greener./The roots of flowers will plunge between your ribs;/Where you are sleeping the grass will grow higher;/In God's hands everything serves!)

The sudden introduction of God's presence seems somewhat unconvincing, especially given Gautier's lack of religious faith, nor does the narrator believe the worm's optimistic proclamation. He concludes the scene with three powerful lines that would one day inspire Baudelaire's "La Cloche fêlée" ("The Cracked Bell"):

Et, me suivant partout, mille cloches fêlées,
Comme des voix de mort, me jetaient par volées
Les râlements du glas.

(And following me everywhere, a thousand cracked church bells,/Like the voices of the dead, pealed out at me/The death rattle of their knell.)

The poem ends in a nihilistic vision. Heaven has no power of salvation. Our century "weeps and writhes in its death throes like a pale old man." Gautier's optimistic idea that life comes from death as soaring cathedral towers emerge from shadowy foundations breaks down completely.

Nor does the last of these three poems do anything to change the tone. Entitled "La Mort dans la vie" ("Death in Life"), it in no way tries to create the idea of an endless cycle of life and death from which new life emerges. On the contrary, it is a hymn to the collapse of all ideals and illusions. Gautier first presents Faust, who announces that having fathomed all knowledge and found it empty, we must turn to love. Whereupon Don Juan appears to proclaim that love turns to ashes and that wisdom is the answer. Next we have a glimpse of Napoleon, who tells us that he dreamed of action and glory only to find that goal, too, vain. Even Nature cannot preserve us from decay and death. The tone is perhaps best exemplified by the following stanza:

> Je vis que d'os blanchis la terre était couverte,
> Froide neige de morts, où nulle plante verte,
> Nulle fleur ne germait;
> Que ce sol n'était fait que de poussière d'homme,
> Et qu'un peuple à remplir Thèbes, Palmyre et Rome
> Etait là qui dormait.

(I saw that the earth was covered with whitened bones,/Cold snow with the dead, where no green plant,/No flower grew;/That the ground was made up of man's dust,/And that a nation big enough to populate Thebes, Palmyra and Rome was sleeping there.)

With such a totally despairing vision ending the first section of the volume that had started out with more optimism, the reader is uncertain what to expect as he proceeds to the fifty-six "poésies diverses." Will they revert to the original idea that something positive can emerge from death, or will they, too, be nihilistic in tone? The answer is that both visions are present simultaneously, a fact that should not surprise us when we realize that the fifty-six poems were written anywhere from 1833 to 1838, and many were written before "Portail." We may eliminate perhaps one-third of them as having little to do with this question. They are pieces of occasional love poetry, inspired by la Cydalise or Victorine of the Impasse du Doyenné, and there are some descriptive exercises. Among the others there are three, and three of the most important, which suggest the idea that Baudelaire was to take so much further. They are "Ténèbres" ("Shadows"), "Magdalena" ("Magdalene"), and "Le Sommet de la tour" ("The Top of the Tower").

In "Ténèbres" the narrator speaks of poets who endlessly pursue a distant El Dorado without ever reaching it, and he senses how wonderful it would be to attain one's goal. We remember that in *Maupin* Albert had not dared to descend into the depths of the human heart but had remained "on the top step." Now Gautier once again suggests that to descend into watery chaos, rather than to try to soar directly upward, might be the wiser course:

> Il est beau qu'un plongeur, comme dans les ballades,
> Descende au gouffre amer chercher la coupe d'or,
> Et perce triomphant les vitreuses arcades.

(It is beautiful to see a diver, as in ballads,/Descend into the bitter abyss to seek the golden cup,/And triumphantly penetrate the glasslike archways [of the sea].)

Should one be triumphant in one's quest, then "dream and action" are united and a moment of epiphany reached. One is able

> D'arrêter, quand on veut, la Fortune et sa roue,
> Et de sentir, la nuit, quelque baiser royal
> Se suspendre en tremblant aux fleurs de votre joue.

(To stop, when one wishes to, Fortune and its wheel,/And to feel, at night, a royal kiss/Trembling on the bloom of one's cheek.)

In "Magdalena," inspired by the Rubens painting in the Cathedral of Antwerp, Gautier muses on the nature of Christ and Mary Magdalene. To find truth, he concludes:

> O poètes! allez prier à cet autel . . .
> Regardez le Jésus et puis la Madeleine,
> Plongez-vous dans votre âme, et rêvez au doux bruit
> Que font en s'éployant les ailes de la nuit.

(O poets! Go and pray at that altar,/Look at Jesus and Mary Magdalene,/Plunge into the depths of your own soul, and dream as you listen to the gentle noise/That the wings of night make as they unfold.)

Then, he promises,

A vos yeux, un moment, soulèvera le voile,
Et dans un long soupir l'orgue murmurera
L'ineffable secret que ma bouche taira.

(Before your eyes, for a moment, the veil will be lifted,/And with a deep sigh the organ will murmur/The ineffable secret that my mouth will not speak.)

Finally, the last of these three poems, "Le Sommet de la tour," consciously picks up the imagery of "Portail," with which Gautier opened his volume. Once again he talks about the necessity of descending underground, "digging like a miner in [his] solitary vein," avoiding springtime and flowers outside as he lays the foundation of his poetic edifice.

But these brief moments, for all their intensity, are exceptional, and "Magdalena" explains why. Pondering the mystery of Jesus, the poet cries out:

O mystère d'amour! ô mystère profond!
Abîme inexplicable où l'esprit se confond!
Qui de nous osera, philosophe ou poète,
Dans cette sombre nuit plonger avant la tête?

(O mystery of love! O deep mystery!/Inexplicable abyss in which the psyche is confounded!/Who of us will dare, philosopher or poet,/To plunge our head into this dark night?)

Gautier is confessing himself to be too weak to embark upon the quest. By refusing to plunge into the unknown, he avoided its dangers, but he also failed to reap the reward of insight that comes to the truly visionary spirit. As a consequence, in most of the poems of this collection, Gautier reverts to his usual technique of setting in opposition a world of darkness and death to one of light and life, and then pessimistically proclaiming the triumph of death in this world. In "Thébaïde" (the title refers to the solitary retreats of the early Christians in the region west of Thebes) Gautier has a final vision of the annihilation of the self and its assimilation into unsentient nature:

Mes pieds prendraient racine et je redeviendrais arbre.
(My feet would sprout roots, and I would become a tree again.)

To conclude, during the 1830's Gautier used his fiction and poetry at least in part as a vehicle of self-discovery. He could see the luminous side of his desires and the darker aspect of existence, but he could not quite integrate them. As far as his poetic technique is concerned, it still floundered badly on many occasions. No doubt Gautier, who had good taste, sensed his own inadequacies, for in "Onuphrius" he had created a metaphor to express his frustrations as a poet. The hero, still dreaming but no longer buried alive, recites poetry to a gathering of people in a salon. But only he and the Devil can see what is happening. As he recites, his words become congealed in the air; the Devil seizes them with a net and substitutes inferior verse, which the audience then hears. The startling image owes much to the "Frozen Words" of Rabelais (one of Gautier's favorite authors), but Gautier gives it his own twist. More generally, the poet's inability either to abandon or to reach his ideal was troubling him to such an extent that he could not bring his art fully under control. Curiously, a trip that he made to Spain in 1840 was to help him achieve a greater degree of integration in both his personality and his art.

II Voyage en Espagne

Théophile was already predisposed to be attracted to Spain by his dream of a warm, exotic paradise, and in 1840 he was ecstatic when he got the opportunity to visit the country that was becoming so popular among the Romantics. For some years he had been a friend of Eugène Piot, who had lived for a time in the Impasse du Doyenné. Piot was by temperament a bibliophile and a collector of curios. He was also a businessman. He had the idea that Spain, ravaged by civil war at the time, would be an ideal place to pick up valuable *objets d'art* — daggers, tapestries, etc. which could be resold for a handsome profit in Paris.[3] While Piot was a good judge of curios, he felt the need to have with him an expert on painting, and his friend Gautier, already established as an art critic, seemed the perfect choice. For his part, Gautier saw that he could publish in *La Presse* periodic accounts of his trip which he would send back to Paris, and he surmised that he could bring out an entire volume upon his return to France. Since Gautier had no money, Piot paid for all the expenses of the trip, but Gautier signed a few promissory notes just in case the trip turned out to be a financial disaster. The two men were optimistic, however, and left in high spirits on May 5, 1840, planning to be gone for several months.

Their trip took them down through the center of Spain, and they returned from Cadiz to France by boat. Unfortunately for both of them, the trip did turn out to be a financial disaster. The only Murillos to be had were pitiful forgeries, and Toledo no longer made the sixteenth-century style daggers so dear to the Romantic heart. Gautier found himself obliged to reimburse Piot 7,500 francs and had to borrow to pay off his debt. Having blithely assumed that the trip would cost him nothing, he always felt a bit cheated by Piot's strict business approach, but the poet never did have much common sense when it came to practical matters, and he continued to think highly enough of his friend to dedicate to him the volume that told the story of their trip. The book appeared in 1843 under the title *Tra los montes*, bad Spanish for *Across the Mountains*. It was soon rebaptized *Voyage en Espagne*, the title it bears today.

Voyage en Espagne can be appreciated at more than one level. It can be understood as a kind of nineteenth-century Michelin Guide, an attempt to inform the bourgeois public in France about details of life in the Iberian peninsula. But Gautier was also trying to achieve something much more personal. He was trying to come to grips with that problem which had been troubling him for years: how could he reconcile the realities of his finite being with the ideal he longed for so passionately? Now he had the opportunity to try to reach a paradise that actually seemed to exist. The trip would reveal first whether his ideal was real or illusory, and even more, although Gautier may not have been fully aware of it when he set out, the trip would force him to examine his own being and try to integrate his personality, for no person can live through the severe testing that comes with an attempt to achieve his heart's desire without making discoveries about his own identity.

Because seeking one's identity is a solitary inner search, most stories of heroic quests show us the hero alone. A Captain Ahab may be surrounded by his crew, but no one could be more isolated. Gautier's narrative was also to take on the form of an archetypal quest, and to that end Gautier omitted some details and even changed others in order to create a coherent work of fiction out of the random events of life. In many ways Gautier's narrative resembles a work of confessional fiction like Chateaubriand's *René*. Both are autobiographical, at least in part; both are accounts of the desperate attempts of a hero to find a solution to life, and both are structured around a quest.[4]

In the section on *La Comédie de la mort* we described in general terms the patterns of quest literature. It is appropriate now to go into greater detail concerning this type of fiction, and in this connection we can do no better than to use Joseph Campbell's schematic outline, as given in *The Hero with a Thousand Faces.*[5] The hero appears to be an ordinary man living in the ordinary, real world, or "the world of common day," to use Campbell's term. He receives a call to adventure. This call may come from any chance event. If he decides to accept the challenge, he must cross a threshold and enter a "region of supernatural wonder." Because he must encounter chaos and death in their many forms in this underworld, he must have the divine protection of Providence if he is to succeed. A false hero, who claims to be more courageous or virtuous than he actually is, will fail the test and often be destroyed. But if he proves worthy, he faces an ultimate test, wins a victory, and lays claim to the treasure. The treasure takes innumerable forms in literature, but in its psychological sense, it is ultimately the treasure of self-knowledge. With new understanding of self comes power, so that now the hero is in a position to return to his people "to bestow boons on his fellow men." Naturally, every quest narrative varies the basic pattern to some extent. The action may be supernatural as in Celtic legends or juvenile as in Robert Louis Stevenson's *Treasure Island.* It may even be parodied as in Voltaire's *Candide,* but the underlying patterns change little. Gautier had only to make sure that in the telling of his personal quest he did not destroy the usefulness of *Voyage en Espagne* as a travel guide.

One problem remains to be solved before we join Gautier on his pilgrimage. During and after the trip he wrote forty-three poems inspired by events and scenes of his experience. They were published in 1845 under the title *España.* René Jasinski has remarked perceptively that the poems in this volume continue and rework the prose narration rather than being a truly independent creation.[6] We agree, and so rather than deal with the volume separately, we prefer to discuss the more important poems in the context of the episodes that inspired them. The *Voyage* is complete without them, but they do highlight and emphasize many of the key motifs of Gautier's quest.

As the narrative begins, we note immediately that Gautier has suppressed any mention of the commercial aspects of his venture. This omission is a good example of Gautier's process of transforming fact into fiction. Probably even without knowing that he was doing it, he was making his protagonist seem more heroic and was creating a reason for his trip that conformed to the typical pattern of quests where the call to adventure can be inspired by the most trivial of causes. "A few weeks ago (April, 1840)," he began, "I had said offhand: 'I'd like to go to Spain!' Five or six days later, my friends had removed the prudent conditional . . . and were repeating to everybody that I was about to take a trip to Spain. To this assertion they added a question: 'When are you leaving?' I answered without realizing what I was letting myself in for: 'In a week.' "[7] And so, as is so often the case, the hero sets out, still unsure of the precise nature of the treasure he is seeking. The season of the year is springtime, the season of hope and renewal, and he leaves Paris in high spirits.

It quickly becomes clear as one begins reading *Voyage en Espagne* that Gautier's quest consists of a whole series of minor episodes, more or less complete in themselves, but whose function is to prepare the last and most important experience. The pattern of each of the early encounters is identical. One leaves a secure, known place, travels through a wilderness where death surrounds the hero, and arrives at some kind of treasure. In each case the experience turns out not to be the ultimate one but merely a preparation for the last and greatest revelation.

This pattern emerged while Gautier was still in France. As far south as Angoulême little was new. Gautier was still in the world of common day, but "south of Angoulême, the terrain changes" (p. 5). He leaves the familiar world and enters the *landes,* or deserted moors, so typical of southwestern France. The hero has reached the sterile wastelands. Emerging from this desolation, he arrives in Bordeaux, his first main stopping point. One might suppose that this city could contain the treasure that our hero is seeking. Bordeaux has a grandeur that seeks to rival Paris, but its geometrical order, created by a predominantly neoclassical architecture, seemed sterile and lifeless to Gautier. The city even gave him the impression of being depopulated. The reality behind the façade of Bordeaux was not the "rather pretty" cathedral, but the crypt of the Saint-Michel Tower. In this underground crypt bodies had been preserved in almost mummified fashion, and Gautier went down among the dead. This theme of descent into an underworld is of course a vital one in any archetypal quest. Should a hero refuse the descent and, like Icarus, try to fly directly up to Heaven, he invites destruction, for he has not dared to test himself in the crucible. In the crypt of the Saint-Michel Tower Gautier accepted the descent among the dead, but he found the experience appalling. When a hero crosses the threshold, all known order is abolished. Quaking rocks, the *symplegades,* announced the presence of a chaotic world to the questing Jason. Medieval demons — evil symbols of the abolition of God's ordered cosmos — guarded the gates to Hell in the medieval theater. Here, the stability of objects was abolished by a trick of lighting. The flickering gleams of the lanterns created a fantasmagoric world where everything seemed hallucinatory. Arriving among the corpses, Gautier encountered death, where flesh was crumbling to dust and skulls grimaced in mockery of the living. He had already presented death as grotesque in *La Comédie de la mort*. Here his worst fears were reinforced: "twisted, grimacing faces, heads with the flesh half peeled off, half-open sides that reveal, through the grillwork of the ribs, lungs that were dried and withered like sponges" (p. 11). As the high point of horror Gautier saw a dead child in his coffin: "His fingernails were sunk into the palms of his hands; his tendons were as taut as the strings of a violin; his knees twisted at convulsive angles; his head was thrown violently backward" (p. 11). Gautier concluded that the child had been buried alive and was so distressed that he fled from the crypt. He had encountered death there, but he certainly had not conquered it.

So he sets out again, this time for Spain itself. Once again he leaves the known — Bordeaux — for the unknown. The *landes* soon reappear, "sadder and more desolate than ever" (p. 14). The pine trees bleed in this wasteland, for they are tapped for their resin. But Gautier anthropomorphizes them in his prose narrative so that they become people dying. He is so struck by the vision that he writes a poem, "Le Pin des Landes" ("The Pine on the Moors"), to dramatize the scene:

> On ne voit en passant par les Landes désertes,
> Vrai Sahara français, poudré de sable blanc,
> Surgir de l'herbe sèche et des flaques d'eau vertes,
> D'autre arbre que le pin avec sa plaie au flanc.

(Passing through the deserted moors,/A true French Sahara, powdered with white sand,/One sees rising from the dry grass and from the pools of green stagnant water/No other tree but the pine with a wound in its side.)

In the poem Gautier goes on to compare the wounded tree to the poet, who gives of himself so that others may reap the benefits. The idea had been made popular by Musset in "La Nuit de mai" and was by now a Romantic commonplace.

But in the prose narrative the scene remains unrelievedly bleak.

As the narrator-hero progresses toward the south, he notes that the cold becomes not less but more intense. A rise in elevation explains this phenomenon on the realistic level, but on the mythic plane the nearer one gets to one's treasure, the more dangerous the trip becomes. One must go through Hell to reach Heaven, as Dante and the Apostle's Creed make clear. Gautier began to notice that the very vegetation looked grotesque. Deformed tree branches and brackish pools all suggested a demonic wasteland, but beyond he could just barely perceive the line of the blue horizon of the ocean. The ideal was beckoning from the end of the dangerous path. But unfortunately no treasure at all awaited Gautier in the last French town, Bayonne. Like Bordeaux, it seemed depopulated; the city looked horrible; even the church steeple was squat and clumsy. Bayonne was merely another part of the wasteland.

Now Spain lay directly ahead. It is customary, if the hero of a quest has the blessing of Providence, for him to receive some aid, some magic talisman to preserve him from harm, before he crosses the threshold. Gautier's only help came in the form of advice from the local populace. They warned him that the Spaniards eat little, that bandits are numerous, and that he should be certain to take a lot of food and ammunition with him. But whether "Providence" was on his side or whether he was just lucky, Gautier was never attacked by bandits and completed his entire trip without serious problems. Perhaps the narrator was not enough of a true hero for the heavens to bother with him, for rather than being full of resolve at the warnings he received, he confessed to considerable nervousness. But he pushed on. To his surprise, the countryside did not once again become barren, but was charming and picturesque, and in the distance he could see the ocean "gentle and deep" (p. 16). But danger often appears when nature is at its most smiling. Passing through the town of Urrugne, Gautier suddenly spied the inscription on the church steeple clock: *Vulnerant omnes, ultima necat,* "Each hour wounds, the last one kills." For the first time on his trip, the theme of the passage of time appears in explicit form. As we remarked at the beginning of this chapter, its close association with death is hardly a novelty in Western culture, but each person must learn each truth of life for himself, and learn them at an emotional as well as intellectual level. When this happens, what has seemed but a platitude before now appears as a revelation. Gautier, who had already known that time flees without recall, now felt the emotional impact of that motto inscribed upon the church. It seemed to be a personal statement meant for him, and he was so moved by the experience that he composed a poem "L'Horloge" ("The Clock") to express his anguish:

> Mais sur l'humble cadran regardé par hasard,
> Comme les mots de flamme aux murs de Balthazar,
> Comme l'inscription de la porte maudite,
> En caractères noirs une phrase est écrite;
> Quatre mots solennels, quatre mots de latin,
> Où tout homme en passant peut lire son destin:
> "Chaque heure fait sa plaie et la dernière achève!"[8]

The next to last line of the passage cited above shows that Gautier has grasped another of the truths that each man must learn as he travels through life, that is, that his quest is the quest of every man.

After all this solemn preparation for the passage into Spain, the crossing of the frontier turned out to be anticlimactic. While Irun was different from a French town, still no danger lurked, the countryside was pleasant, the food good. Perhaps the Spain of Gautier's dreams would turn out to be both real and accessible. But no treasure of value can be achieved easily. Arriving in Vittoria in a cold wind, which should have served as a warning, Gautier had an unpleasant shock. Enthusiastic about the idea of seeing authentic boleros and fandangos, he went to see his first Spanish dancers. The disillusionment was total. The two dancers were old, tired, and decrepit. They had hardly any energy, and the woman twitched like a dead frog shocked by an electric current, while the man shivered in the corner like a "gravedigger burying himself" (p. 30). The macabre bolero seemed a living recreation of the ghastly specters in the crypt of the Saint-Michel Tower. Gautier was witnessing a vivid demonstration of the meaning of the warning on the Urrugne clock tower. Nothing lasts forever, not even a culture that has reached its perfect expression.

This grisly experience was followed closely by another lesson in the tyranny of time. Old Castille seemed to be populated primarily by crones as old as the province itself. They were in Gautier's eyes so ugly and repulsive that Macbeth's witches seemed young and pretty in comparison. As he journeyed south, the terrain became more and more desolate, a fact that did nothing to improve his morale. But when Gautier arrived in Burgos, he was overwhelmed by the beauty of the cathedral, and he praised it ecstatically: "On looking upwards, one can see a kind of dome . . . an abyss full of sculptures, arabesques, statues, colonnades . . . that makes you dizzy. One could look for two years and not see everything. . . . It's as gigantic as a pyramid and as delicate as a lady's earring, and it is impossible to imagine that such a filigree could sustain itself in the air for centuries" (p. 38). To Gautier such beauty was precious. He exhorted the Spaniards to "kill each other off if they must" in their civil war. "In ten thousand years, people will have forgotten your civil discord, and the future will know you were great only because of a few marvelous fragments unearthed by the excavations" (p. 53).

Gautier had not yet learned, however, that the real treasures are those of self-discovery. Even the beautiful cathedral, whose art would, he thought, outlive contemporary culture, failed to bring him peace, for the ravages of time could be found even there. While the art appeared eternal, where were the men who had built such a marvel? "Is their race lost forever?" Gautier asked. "And are we, who brag about our civilization, only decrepit barbarians?" (p. 39). The very perfection of this ancient art brought home to him the inevitable rise and decline of civilizations. As if saddened by his experience in the cathedral, he went off to the Monastery *(Cartuja)* of Miraflores, situated on a hilltop. Here he discovered to his surprise that death did not always seem ghastly and frightening. "The cemetery," he wrote, "is shaded by two or three large cypress trees. . . . This enclosure contains [the bodies of] four hundred and nineteen monks who have died here since the monastery was founded. . . . They lie in no particular order, humble in death as they were in life. This anonymous cemetery has something calm and silent about it which reposes the soul; a fountain in the middle of it mourns with silvery tears these forgotten dead; I drank a swallow of this water that was filtered through the bones of these holy people; it was pure and cold as death" (p. 54).[9]

Gautier's delight in the calmness of the scene indicates that he had arrived at one of those critical moments on the quest when the hero is tempted to abandon his voyage in exchange for repose or pleasure. Even Ulysses dallied for a time with Calypso, and his sailors were only too willing to forget their responsibilities among the lotus eaters. What appealed to Gautier was merely escapism. He envied those monks who had managed to retreat from the turmoil of life in order to create their own closed society high above most other men.

On leaving Burgos for Madrid, the terrain became sterile as he headed south. He saw villages lying in ruins; the city of Valladolid, whose population had shrunk from perhaps 100,000 to but 20,000, looked dead and deserted. The wasteland housed little but vipers, owls, and lizards, and a chill wind howled across the Castillian plateau. But then the road moved up into the mountains, and once up in the clear, pure air, Gautier felt a sudden, exhilarating sense of intoxication: "I felt myself so light, so joyous and so full of enthusiasm that I shrieked and scampered about like a young kid; I felt the desire to hurl myself into all these magical abysses. . . . I would have liked to tumble down in the rushing streams and . . . to blend in with nature, to melt like an atom into this immensity" (p. 68). Gautier had come to another of those moments when the hero is tempted to abandon his quest. Here it takes the form of abdicating his own humanity. In order to overcome the tyranny of time and death, he longed to become one with unsentient nature which, unlike man, can renew itself eternally. It is significant that Gautier felt this blissful illusion once again when he was up, away from mankind, reality, and finitude. One of the poems of *España*, "Les Yeux bleus de la montagne" ("The Blue Eyes of the Mountain"), celebrates the perfection and beauty to be found far away from men. As the poem is brief, we give it in its entirety.

On trouve dans les monts des lacs de quelques toises,
Purs comme des cristaux, bleus comme des turquoises,
Joyaux tombés du doigt de l'ange Ithuriel,
Où le chamois craintif, lorsqu'il vient pour y boire,
S'imagine, trompé par l'optique illusoire,
Laper l'azur du ciel.
Ces limpides bassins, quand le jour s'y reflète,
Ont comme la prunelle une humide paillette;
Et ce sont les yeux bleus, au regard calme et doux,
Par lesquels la montagne en extase contemple,
Forgeant quelque soleil dans le fond de son temple,
Dieu, l'ouvrier jaloux![10]

In the universe of this brief poem, man is excluded from the perfect harmony of God and Nature, and surely Gautier must have wanted to stop time and stay there, as he had in the cemetery of the monastery, but there was no choice but to continue on his way, and soon he was out of the mountains and back down in the barren plains that surround Madrid, then on into the city where he stayed several weeks.

Life in the capital turned out not to please Gautier very much. He had the good fortune to get to know upper-class Spaniards (his literary reputation had preceded him), but his account of the soirées, or *tertulias,* to which he was invited was not a joyous one. He complained that no food was served, but even worse, he noted, the Spaniards had lost all sense of "Spanishness." The aristocratic women dressed *à la française,* and Gautier was scornful of the results. He claimed that their clothing was no longer Spanish and yet not really French either. He was equally exasperated that no one wished to dance the traditional national dances and only did so — rather unwillingly — to humor their eccentric visitor. Gautier's command of Spanish was not very great; he had not studied it until his trip began, but it was not his limited vocabulary that explains his social failures. Gautier knew of course that a foreigner with a poor grasp of the language could not penetrate to the heart of a culture in a few days. As he commented after a later trip to Constantinople when he was again criticized for not getting "into" the culture: "I am a foreigner; I came to visit their city, which is famous everywhere for its picturesque character and beauty. I walked all around, I examined everything, I entered buildings open to Christians; I put my observations down in my book; I made every effort for it to be rigorously exact, well written, witty and amusing. I succeeded fairly well, and it was not easy. . . . How could I know what the Turks think, since we don't speak the same language, since they live behind closed doors, and are distrustful, reserved, and carefully keep Europeans at a distance?"[11] To a lesser extent the same problems faced Gautier in Spain, but it was not, we repeat, his inability to speak the language that was the true barrier to his acceptance, but his refusal to face one simple reality: Spain was not the exotic land of his dreams. In his poem "A Madrid," he tried to recreate some of the savagery that he believed Spanish women possessed by showing an elegant marquise admiring the macabre details of a sculpted head of John the Baptist, but the *Voyage* sees Spanish culture only in its death throes. To Gautier these manifestations of cultural death were not so much horrible as shameful, because in his eyes the Spaniards had not been forced to abandon the old ways and become pseudo-French. Little by little Gautier was learning that death takes many forms and has many moods. It appeared horrible in Bordeaux, serene in Miraflores, and shameful in Madrid.

Still another face of death awaited him when he took a brief side trip out of the capital to visit the Escurial. He approached the forbidding sanctuary of Philip II with the usual Romantic preconceptions, for the Escurial had long had a European reputation as a grim and somber place. He no doubt thought it fitting that the approaches to the edifice were even more desolate than usual for Castille. A few steps from the door Gautier smelled "the odor of stale holy water" (p. 128), and once inside he felt utterly crushed by the lifeless weight of the building. Its massive, unadorned architecture was appalling. The very stones seemed sullen to him, and the air was permeated with boredom and stagnation. The crypt was cold and deadly. Even the church of the Escurial provided no relief: "One is so beaten down, so crushed by the domination of an inflexible and dismal power, that prayer is useless" (pp. 129 - 30). To portray death and evil (the Romantics saw Philip as a wicked king) as heavy, cold, and immobile was of course not new with Gautier, the Romantics, or others. In his *Inferno* Dante had reserved these same characteristics for the very pit of Hell. Gautier left the Escurial with a vast sense of relief, feeling in the open air that he was actually being reborn to life.

The only encounter with death that seemed to offer some kind of hope to Gautier came in Madrid when he spent an afternoon at the bullfights. As he entered the stands, he became dizzy from the dazzling sunlight, which seemed to blur all outlines and forms; the noise, too, was unsettling. It seemed to Gautier a haze of noise *(un brouillard de bruit)*. He had once again left the ordinary world and crossed a threshold into another — this time a literal — arena of testing. As the crowd tensed for the appearance of the first bull, Gautier felt his heart gripped by an invisible hand; his ears were ringing, and a cold chill went through him. "It was one of the strongest emotions that I have ever experienced" (p. 79), he recalled. Death in one of its ugliest forms was soon thrust before his eyes when one of the horses was badly gored by the bull. Gautier was deeply moved: "I had already seen at Montfaucon what strange fantastic forms death gives to horses: it is certainly the animal whose dead bodies are the saddest to see. The head, so nobly and purely sculptured, [is now] flattened out by the finger of nothingness" (p. 82). But when the moment came for the bull to die, Gautier seemed to sense that the very confrontation with death could give meaning to life. True, if the killing is clumsily done, or if the animal is merely disabled, "it is no longer a combat but a disgusting butchery" (p. 87), but if circumstances are favorable, the scene is "worth all of Shakespeare's plays; in a few seconds one of the actors will be killed. . . . The man has no protection; he is dressed as for a ball. . . . In this duel the bull has every material advantage: he has two horns sharp as daggers, an immense thrust, and the anger of a brute who has no sense of danger; but the man has his sword and his courage, and twelve thousand people watching him. . . . As the bull falls forward on his knees after a clean sword thrust, he seems to be recognizing the superiority of his adversary" (pp. 83 - 84). Gautier was spellbound. He had seen a demonstration of a fundamental truth. He sensed its power but did not quite grasp its significance. All men must die, but it is in facing the reality of death with courage that man gives himself dignity. The lesson of the bullring is that we are free to decide whether to confront the ultimate with bravery or cowardice. It was the real treasure that Madrid contained, but Gautier did not have the insight to know it.

Instead, he longed for the perfect woman. We saw above that he was disillusioned by the upper-class women he met, but he did not despair. What he was seeking was a perfect *manola.* A *manola,* Gautier explained, is the Spanish equivalent of a *grisette,* the young, coquettish working girl. "Which of you has known the manolas of Madrid? She is better than the grisette of Bordeaux, better than the girl who makes hats in Paris. She has the vivacity of the serpent, the grace of a bird: — an outfit of silk and satin, shining in the sun, showing off the most elegant of figures. Her face . . . is witty, ardent, teasing; she is fire, flame, the passion of the moment, the royal whim, the burning caprice."[12] For *España* he composed one brief poem in the *manola's* honor. He never really found this idealized person, of course, and noted sadly in *Voyage* that the *manolas* were disappearing from Madrid. Those few who were left no longer dressed in colorful fashion. For days he sought "a pure-bred manola" (p. 93) in every nook and cranny of the city. Once, if we may believe his account, he saw one for the first and last time disappearing around the corner. One may well suspect that the episode was invented as a metaphor to express his feeling that his ideals were elusive and vanishing.

The series of negative experiences in Madrid seemed to have shaken Gautier considerably, for he appeared more than glad to leave the city for a short trip to Toledo to see the Alcazar. But the architecture of the old fortress only intensified his despondency. The building was beautiful, "with a great stairway of fairylike elegance, with columns, ramps, and marble steps already half broken, leading up to a door that opened onto an abyss, for this part of the building has crumbled away. This admirable stairway . . . which ends up at nothing has something pretentious and odd about it" (p. 144).

Gautier compared it to the drawings of Piranesi, who was popular at that time among the Romantics.[13] Piranesi's engravings show endless arches and stairs which create the illusion of a three-dimensional labyrinth that never really leads anywhere. This architecture seemed to Gautier a kind of symbol for man's life. Filled with "immeasurable sadness," he even began to doubt his own identity (p. 145). He spoke of feeling "absent" — we would say alienated — from himself, as if he found himself in a dream from which he would soon awaken. But this rare moment of introspection did not lead to enlightenment. He moved back from the precipice of his own inner being — something that a Hugo, a Baudelaire, or a Rimbaud would not have done — and took refuge in describing the perfection of the Cathedral of Toledo. Finding an order in art that he could not find in his life, he reveled in the "totally homogeneous and complete style. . . . Stained glass windows sparkling with emeralds, sapphires and rubies . . . filter a soft and mysterious light that predisposes toward religious raptures" (p. 150).

Perhaps Gautier was obscurely aware that he was failing as a genuine hero by running away from self-discovery. At least, at this point he begins to recount legends about another false hero, King Rodrigue of eighth-century Spain. According to the story, Rodrigue seduced Florinda, the daughter of Count Julian; the latter was outraged and brought in the Moors to help him avenge his daughter's honor. Rodrigue lost a key battle and killed himself shortly afterwards. Gautier also tells another story about this same king. According to it, Rodrigue broke into a taboo underground crypt seeking riches only to discover that his act of desecration magically brings about the Moorish invasion of Spain. In both stories Rodrigue suffers from personal greed and must pay the penalty for his selfishness. Gautier was perhaps not selfish as was the ancient Spanish king, but he was failing in his quest nonetheless.

He had one last opportunity to find the treasure of self-knowledge. After returning from Toledo to Madrid, he set out directly for Andalusia and its beautiful city Grenada. All along, he had felt that beyond the Sierra Morena lay his paradise. In Vittoria when he had seen the wretched dancers, he hoped to find good ones in Madrid, but once in the capital, he became convinced that the truth and poetry of Spain lay farther to the south.

As was typical of each new phase of his quest, Gautier set out across desolate land. South of Madrid in July the sky at noon seemed like molten metal; there were no trees anywhere and no water in the dried-up creeks. At forks in the road dubious crosses "stretched out their sinister arms" (p. 180). Gautier captured this intense desolation in one of the most important poems of *España,* "In deserto." The poet evokes

> Les pitons des sierras, les dunes du désert
> Où ne pousse jamais un seul brin d'herbe vert;
> Les monts aux flancs zébrés de tuf, d'ocre et de marne,
> Et que l'éboulement de jour en jour décharne,
> Les grès pleins de micas papillotant aux yeux. . . .

(The peaks of the sierras, the dunes of the desert/Where a blade of grass never grows;/The mountains with their slopes jagged with tuffa, ocre and marl,/And which rock slides make more barren each day,/The sandstone full of mica sparkling before one's eyes. . . .)

But the poem goes on to reveal that Gautier has finally come to understand that the sterile wasteland is also a projection of the poet's own inner aridity, for he adds that all this mineral sterility is "less dry and less desolate to growth than my heart is to passions," and by the end of the poem, we find him begging some "female Moses" to smite the rock of his heart so that others could come and bathe in its life-giving waters.

But no woman came to give his life meaning. If the soldiers escorting the coach could laugh gaily and seemed to enjoy the trip, Gautier was more somber. What stuck in his mind was a scene in the town of Tembleque. Here he and Piot stopped to buy ladies' garters. Suddenly they heard a howling like an angry dog, and when they turned to look, they saw that the sound was produced not by an animal but by a man, a blind beggar with sunken eyes and flattened nose and grotesquely protruding lower jaw. He reminds anyone familiar with French literature of the blind beggar in Flaubert's *Madame Bovary,* and indeed, he serves the same function. A symbol of death, he appears just when feminine sexuality is stressed. So much for salvation by women.

As the convoy approached the mountains that separate Castille from Andalusia, "the stones became rocks . . . thistles six or seven feet high thrust up along the road like the halberds of invisible soldiers" (p. 191). These were the first obstacles in the final series of barriers before crossing the threshold to paradise. The road zigzagged as if to discourage the casual traveler until finally it wound through a pass and there followed a descent into a gorge with vegetation so thick that it was almost impenetrable. But the difficult passage was worth the effort, for Andalusia was indeed a kind of paradise as it opened up before Gautier's delighted eyes. A panorama as vast as the sea was spread beneath him; distant mountain ranges undulated softly; the sun touched hillocks with its gold. Everything was inundated "with a light that must have lit up the Garden of Eden" (p. 194). "Vegetation was everywhere. African aloes, roses with emerald foliage, rose laurels and olive trees abounded and all was in harmony" (p. 195). At Beylen fields of wheat waved gently in the breeze, and snow-capped mountain peaks were dazzling with light. Over and over again Gautier uses the imagery of precious gems to express the perfection of the landscape and reiterates the statement that Andalusia is a "terrestrial paradise" (e.g., p. 210). The dream of his youth had apparently come true.

For Gautier, the Alhambra, situated on hills overlooking Grenada, represented in concentrated form all he loved about southern Spain. "How many hours I spent there," he recalled, "with one leg hanging out over the abyss, telling my eyes to remember each form, each contour of the admirable picture spread out before them, and which they no doubt will never see again" (p. 226). Gautier was so reluctant to leave the Alhambra that he spent several nights there. Nearby at the Generalife there was a rose laurel by a pool. It seemed to incarnate all of Gautier's desires, as one of the poems from *España*, "Le Laurier du généralife," makes clear. After describing the tree by the pool in an initial strophe, the poet makes a revealing comparison:

> Il [le laurier] rougit dans l'azur comme une jeune fille;
> Ses fleurs, qui semblent vivre, ont des teintes de chair.
> On dirait, à le voir sous l'onde qui scintille,
> Une odalisque nue attendant qu'on l'habille,
> Cheveux en pleurs, au bord du bassin au flot clair.
>
> Ce laurier, je l'aimais d'une amour sans pareille;
> Chaque soir, près de lui, j'allais me reposer;
> A l'une de ses fleurs, bouche humide et vermeille,
> Je suspendais ma lèvre, et parfois, ô merveille!
> J'ai cru sentir la fleur me rendre mon baiser.[14]

Gautier had found his Eden, but it was in fact nothing more than what he had found on his way to Madrid when intoxicated with joy in the pure air of the mountains. Then he had wished to melt into nature. Now the ideal woman is incorporated into it. His paradise could exist only without real human beings.

So intense was his desire to escape reality that not long afterwards he fled to a mountain to achieve serenity. Near Grenada the Mulhacén soars to over 11,000 feet above sea level, and Gautier, his friend, a German tourist, and a guide climbed up on horseback to an elevation of 9,000 feet. The German and Piot went on to the top, but Gautier wished to be alone and was far enough above the chaos of humanity below to be satisfied. Nature was pure and perfect. "We made camp below a rock, near a little spring whose water sparkled like diamonds and glittered as it flowed through the emerald grass" (p. 250). Here Gautier saw a bird kill a snake, as if proclaiming that evil must not exist in Eden. Looking down at the landscape, he felt godlike in his sense of superiority. Observing the jumbled hills and valleys below, he wrote: "Nothing gives the idea of chaos, of a universe still in the hands of its Creator, as a range of hills seen from above. You might say that a nation of Titans had tried to build an enormous tower there . . . and that an unknown hand had knocked it down" (p. 252). He had had the same feeling in the Sierra Nevada, according to the testimony of poem XXIII of *España*.

But the hero, as before, was obliged to go down into the city. Here in Grenada he tried desperately to continue his paradise among living people. He even had a colorful suit (like a bullfighter's) made for him in an attempt to be one with the culture, but he succeeded only in making himself ridiculous. Early in his trip he had referred to himself as a man without passion (p. 131), but now he fell wildly in love with a local lady. His effort to become a passionate human being, which we may understand as the effort to give of himself totally, did not meet with success, however, and he was so disillusioned that he avoided mentioning the entire matter in his final narrative.[15] The presence of other people inevitably destroyed his ideals.

Another disappointment awaited him in Andalusia. In Madrid, we remember, he had been struck by the possibility of achieving dignity by facing death with courage in the bullring, but in Malaga, his next stop, he discovered that heroes could easily turn into cowards. Montès, the great bullfighter, dispatched a bull improperly because he was petrified with fear, and the fallen hero was booed by the crowd.

A few days later Gautier arrived in Cordova where he was again reminded of the inevitable passage of time. He visited a Christian church that had been once a pagan temple and then a Moorish mosque. "The first [religion] has disappeared into the abyss of the past along with the civilization it stood for; the second was thrown out of Europe . . . [and] the third, after having reached its apogee, undermined by the spirit of free inquiry, becomes weaker every day, even in countries where it reigns as an absolute sovereign" (p. 312). This sense of loss had become obsessive by the time Gautier reached Seville. He regretted that men no longer understood the soaring faith which built the city's beautiful cathedral, and he meditated on the gruesome painting of Juan Valdés Leal, "Los Dos Cadáveres" ("The Two Cadavers"). This painting shows the rotting bodies of an ecclesiastical bishop and a once handsome knight rotting in a vault. "Finis gloria mundi" is inscribed below, and the strict scales of justice hang above. But Gautier did not describe in detail either this painting or another one by Valdés Leal that he saw in Seville but reserved their fullest treatment for *España*. The reason seems clear enough. Gautier's narrative little by little was beginning to take on a new tone. Up to now he had looked ahead eagerly to the next stage in his journey. Up to now he had described everything with leisurely care and great detail. But now that he had discovered emotionally what his mind had told him, that perfection in human life was impossible and that death must eventually make life tragic, he lost interest in his trip. He continued to provide dutiful descriptions of Jerez and Cadiz, but he was eager now to return to Europe, his "land of common day."

At Cadiz he embarked on a French boat and returned via the Mediterranean. Passing near the coast of Africa, he wondered briefly if the Dark Continent were not the true paradise. Wasn't it the cradle of oriental civilization, the center of Islam, and the dark world of the blacks? To see and pass by, he claimed, was like a torture to him. Although he did soon visit North Africa and later, Italy, Russia, and other countries, his accounts never again quite recaptured the intense excitement of *Voyage en Espagne*, which has a life and vitality — until the final chapters — that set it apart from his other books of travel.

The opening poem of *España*, "Départ," gives the impression of having been written prior to Gautier's departure from Paris. In it the poet denies any intent to find the paradise of his dreams and claims that all he wishes is to get away for a while. But we should not take this explanation too seriously, especially since we know that the poem was written, not before, but during and after his trip. In the words of D. H. Lawrence: "Never trust the artist. Trust the tale."[16] "Départ" is in fact best understood as Gautier's concluding statement about his experiences in Spain, and it is obvious that in his eyes the trip was a failure. His attitude is understandable. He was left with burdensome debts, and even worse, he had discovered that no earthly paradise was possible for human beings. His sense of disappointment is clearly expressed:

> L'objet le plus hideux, que le lointain estompe,
> Prend une belle forme où le regard se trompe.

(The most hideous object, whose outlines are blurred by distance,/Takes on a beautiful form that deceives the eyes.)

Furthermore, an impartial reader can see that in the *Voyage* Gautier had not profited from his many opportunities to learn that one must not see the real and the ideal as polar opposites, but must work through reality, finitude, and even death to achieve a fusion of the two. Yet in the most fundamental sense, Gautier's quest was not a failure. René Jasinski long ago noted that "the Spanish trip marked the decisive moment of [Gautier's] evolution," and he sensed that afterwards Gautier's art had greater clarity, health, and classicism.[17] What had happened was something that often happens in quest literature. The real treasure is, ironically, not what the hero expects it to be. Gautier had sought his paradise in vain, but the very act of discovering that paradises do not exist led to that self-knowledge which, as we mentioned at the beginning of this chapter, constitutes the real treasure. Gautier in fact achieved a new understanding of the limits of human aspirations. He did not, of course, abandon his interest in the absolute in literature, as is obvious from all his later writing. But he did abandon the frenetic search for it *in this world*, and this new attitude no doubt explains why Jasinski feels that 1840 marks the end of Gautier's Romantic phase. Henceforth, Gautier would be content to search for perfection in art alone. While the Spanish experience increased his pessimism, it also gave him a kind of serenity — or at the very least a sense of resignation — that he had not known before. He had come out of the uncertainties of the 1830's and formed his definitive view of existence.

III *Epilogue: Gautier's Spanish Vaudeville*

When Gautier returned to Paris, he not only polished the text of *Voyage en Espagne* and gave his poetry, *España*, its final form, he also composed (with the aid of a collaborator) a vaudeville with almost the identical title. *Un Voyage en Espagne* had its premiere at the Théâtre des Variétés on September 21, 1843. The play had a good run of thirty-four performances. The plot is standard fare for a nineteenth-century French vaudeville. The central character is called Désiré Reniflard, a comic name, for *renifler* means to sniff out or to sniff around. He is a rather simple-minded but enthusiastic young Parisian who has gone to Spain for its local color. He dreams of serenading beautiful Spanish women, of Toledo daggers, of everything, in short, that Gautier himself had dreamed before leaving Paris for the Iberian peninsula. Désiré has some of the experiences that Gautier had — bad food and poor lodging — and he has another that Gautier had actually hoped he would have — an encounter with bandits. On top of all this, he becomes involved in an amorous intrigue. It seems that the heroine, Doña Catalina, is constantly watched by her guardian, Don Inigo, and so cannot be free to love Don Ramon de la Cruz, who loves her. To deceive her guardian, she pretends to love Désiré. The poor unsuspecting Frenchman is eventually fooled by everybody and is even accused of political treachery by the various factions vying for control of the country. Of course, everything ends happily for Doña Catalina and Don Ramon, and Désiré is saved from hanging at the last moment.

It is obvious that the play is a self-parody on Gautier's part.[18] What is most notable is its lighthearted tone and the absence of any bitterness. Gentle self-mockery can come only when one has resolved inner tensions and when one can freely and fully accept one's identity. Gautier's vaudeville is further proof that the poet had achieved greater maturity and serenity thanks to his Spanish trip.

CHAPTER 5

Plays and Ballets

Théophile Gautier's involvement with the theater was not restricted to his vaudeville on Spain. He was well aware that box-office hits could make a man wealthy in a way that poetry and even journalism could not, and — on a less material plane — he was no doubt seeking critical acclaim in the theater which might enhance his general reputation in the world of letters. Between the years 1839 and 1850 Gautier wrote all or part of nine different plays. We have already discussed *Un Voyage en Espagne* (1843) in the preceding chapter. We shall omit altogether his drama *La Juive de Constantine* (1846), because the text is generally unavailable. It can be of little interest to the nonspecialist for whom this book is intended. We are also omitting the comedy, *Regardez mais ne touchez pas* (1847), because it was written less by Gautier than by his collaborators, and *Pierrot en Espagne* (1847), because it is only a scenario for a pantomime and one cannot be absolutely certain that Gautier wrote it.[1] Finally, *L'Amour souffle où il veut*, begun in 1850, was never finished. In this chapter we shall treat only his four main plays: *Une Larme du diable* (1839), *Le Tricorne enchanté* (1845), *La Fausse Conversion* (1846), and *Pierrot posthume* (1847). These four plays were included in *Théâtre*, first published in 1872, and are not impossible to find.[2]

The first of the four Gautier wrote entirely on his own. For the others he used what the French call a "carcassier," that is, a specialist in theatrical composition who could make sure that entrances and exits were properly timed and that there was always someone on stage (an important convention of that era). Gautier used a minor dramatist named Paul Siraudin as his principal "carcassier," and apparently the two men worked well and fruitfully together, but critics agree that Siraudin's technical assistance in no way keeps these plays from being Gautier's own creations.

I Une Larme du diable

In *Mademoiselle de Maupin* and in much of his theatrical criticism Gautier had preached in favor of a theater of fantasy. This was all very well, but any deviation from what the mass of theatergoers expected to see could cause problems. Alfred de Musset had already written whimsical, nonrealistic drama that was unappreciated by audiences expecting the standard fare of "well-made" plays. Gautier probably feared that his efforts might have a similar fate. The fear of rejection by an uncomprehending public was strong in him, and he was also alarmed by the possibility of government censorship. At any rate, his first play, *Une Larme du diable* ("The Devil's Tear"), was published in 1839 along with a number of stories that Gautier had already written and was reissuing. The play was destined never to be performed during the author's lifetime.

The date of the play's composition cannot be fixed with any certainty, especially as the manuscript has disappeared, but Professor Book-Senninger believes that it was written some time after Gautier's trip to Belgium in 1836.[3] It is an imitation of a medieval mystery play, a type of drama that became very popular during the fourteenth century. These plays were religious in nature and performed in churches on high festival days. Gautier's play opens in Heaven. God and various celestial figures are busy admiring the innocence, virtue, and piety of two girls on earth named Alix and Blancheflor. Satan interrupts the conversation and suggests that God and his hosts are naive and that he could easily seduce these girls. So a bet is arranged. If Satan loses, he will give up fifty souls presently broiling in Hell; if he wins, he will receive a glass of water to quench his thirst, for the flames of Hell are exceedingly hot. To accomplish his purpose, Satan takes on the form of a handsome young man, and within a very short time, the girls have forgotten their guardian angels (to whom they were to be celestially married after death) and are quivering with very earthly desire and anticipation. The clock eventually runs out on Satan before he can win his wager, but it takes some cheating on the part of the Heavenly forces to defeat the Evil One.

The inspiration for this play has been traced to a considerable number of sources, especially to Goethe's *Faust*. There are also echoes of Alfred de Vigny's epic poem *Eloa*, in which a female angel is seduced by Satan (her name is even mentioned in Gautier's play). On a more abstract or theological level, Professor Book-Senninger sees in the mystical union of the girls' souls with those of their guardian angels a reflection of Swedenborgian mysticism.[4] Perhaps so, but she admits that Satan is a mixture of every kind of literary reminiscence and that the seduction scenes are as old as the hills, so it is probably wiser not to drag the esoteric doctrines of Swedenborg into this nonmystical play.

What, then, is the mystery all about? At one level it can be viewed as a parody of traditional Christianity. God is at times a rather bumbling figure, and Satan is clearly more likeable. Further, the Devil's comments are usually accurate, and one can sense that he is intended to speak many of the truths of the play. A good example is Satan's traditional critique of Paradise. He reminds God that in Heaven one finds only "beggars, idiots, and babies who have died in infancy," whereas in his establishment, things are very different: "It's full of popes, cardinals, emperors, kings . . . and official saints of the Christian calendar." When God becomes angered at this sally and threatens the Devil, Satan mocks him: "Eternal Father, you're getting angry, so you must be in the wrong" (p. 7). We can sense Gautier's own pagan disapproval of Christianity here, and one can well understand why Gautier feared the royal censor.

But there is another, perhaps more important, level to this play, one which is first revealed by an odd detail. Othello and Desdemona — of all people — are in Heaven along with Mary Magdalene and the Virgin Mary. Gautier has included them so that he may more easily bring the discussion in Heaven around to the subject of woman's fidelity to man. When Satan concludes his wager with God, Othello intrudes to announce that all women are treacherous, despite the lesson of Shakespeare's play. Then Mary Magdalene accuses Desdemona of secretly desiring Cassio, refusing to be his mistress only because she feared that a white baby would reveal her infidelity. She adds that "decent women" are all hypocrites anyway, and although Desdemona rejects the accusations, the tone of the play is set. Even God Himself becomes embroiled in the conversation on the merits of women. When Satan boasts that he can seduce the girls and God answers: "Remember Job," Satan has a ready answer: "Job was a man so the matter is entirely different" (p. 8). Gautier seems to be well on his way to forgetting about a theater of fantasy and to turning the play into an antifeminine diatribe.

When the action moves from Heaven to Earth, Satan encounters the two girls, one blonde, one brunette. He calls the first his ideal and the second his reality, but otherwise the motif of Gautier's story

"Celle-ci et celle-là" is ignored. Satan has none of Gautier's own uncertainties about what he wants. The girls appear to be decent enough in an adolescent kind of way, but it is difficult to see in these two cream puffs heroines of any stature. In fact, their superficiality provides us with more evidence of the basically antifeminine nature of the play. Satan develops the idea further. Ever since Eve, he reminds us, women have cuckolded men, and the reason for this practice is, we are told, that girls are uniquely motivated by instinctive sexual desires. When Satan switches missals in church, Blancheflor is immediately fascinated by an erotic picture hidden within the Devil's text. Satan concludes that the three theological virtues cannot compete with the seven deadly sins. Nor does there appear to be any redeeming aspects to woman's love. When Satan points out that one can have two dozen "eternal" love affairs in one year, he is no doubt aiming at men as well as women. When a caterpillar wishes to love a rose, however, Gautier's antifeminism quickly becomes obvious. At first the rose is horrified at this insect's drooling all over her, and Satan explains that the allegorical scene represents a parallel with an old man drooling over a young girl. But when the caterpillar reminds the flower that his drool is silvery and that he wishes to marry her, the rose has a quick change of heart: "You aren't as ugly as I first thought" (p. 24). In other words, a girl will take an old lecher if he is rich enough. She is not even faithful to sexual instincts; she will settle without much difficulty for the pleasures that money can buy.

Curiously, the satire of woman's desire in no way leads Gautier to espouse chastity as a virtue. Woman's eroticism, we gather, is in the nature of things. The physical parts of the two girls actually speak in the play. Alix's breast wishes to be caressed and ultimately filled with milk, and the girls' sex organs worry lest they remain sterile. All is rutting in Nature, and Satan concludes for the author: "What is called lust in the catechism is called love in the world" (p. 41). But there seems to be more weariness than joy in his realization of this fact.

The play does have a superficially happy ending, however, even for Satan who loses his bet, for he sheds a tear of true compassion for the girls along the way. God takes the tear and puts it in a goblet that will eternally renew itself in Hell so that Satan can refresh himself. But this happy finale should not obscure the basic message. If Gautier knows that carnal love is the way of the world and that it is folly for the Church to oppose it, his vision of women and love is so bleak that life offers no salvation. As Satan says, at best it is all a gamble (p. 41). In short, *Une Larme du diable* is a play which preaches both in favor of and against human love, revealing that Gautier's psychological uncertainties in this decade of the 1830's indeed took many forms. It is the same hesitation that made him willing to recognize and loyally support his mistresses and his children born out of wedlock but made him at the same time flee from the permanent ties of marriage.

Before leaving *Une Larme du diable* we must mention that despite all the antifeminism there remain some technical features of the play that put it in the tradition of a theater of fantasy. To have roses and caterpillars, and elsewhere rabbits, speaking is an example of Gautier's revolt against the "well-made" play of his day. But there is an even more interesting detail. Gautier as author appears as a character to talk to the audience about the inadequacy of the play's structure. He confesses that there is a sameness to the seduction scenes that makes him wish he had only one heroine instead of two. If he included them both, he says, it was probably because he felt like imitating the scene in Molière's *Dom Juan* where the hero seduces two village girls. This intrusion by the author underscores the idea that events and characters in the play are not real, that it is all play and illusion. This motif is, of course, a frequent device of twentieth-century theater. So modern, in fact, is Gautier's play that it had to wait until 1897 for his daughter, Judith, to stage it for the first time. She had it performed again in 1910. In 1965 René Clair adapted the play to radio, with the role of Satan played by Gérard Philippe. Finally, one must mention that its American premiere, which this critic had the pleasure of attending, was held in Albuquerque, New Mexico in October 1972 under the direction of Claude Book-Senninger.

II La Fausse Conversion

We shall consider *La Fausse Conversion* next, even if it is not the next play that Gautier wrote, because like *Une Larme du diable* it is written in prose and is primarily a vehicle for satire. It was published in the *Revue des Deux Mondes* on March 1, 1846. Again like *Une Larme du diable* it was not performed during Gautier's lifetime. Judith Gautier had it staged at the Odéon in 1899.

In this one-act play Gautier leaves the medieval period and moves nearer to the present. *La Fausse Conversion* ("The False Conversion") is set in the eighteenth century. As one might expect of an elitist like Gautier, his vision of the preceding century blocks out any glimpse of the social misery that preceded the French Revolution. Influenced in art by painters like Watteau, Boucher, and Fragonard, Gautier preferred to see only the agreeable life of rich aristocrats and complaisant actresses. In an article published in 1836 he mourned the death of the old society, exclaiming: "Where are the intimate suppers, the dances in cozy, secluded houses? . . . Today there are no more aristocrats fighting over actresses as they leave the theater, no more page boys or messengers who give an actor an urgent invitation from a female admirer."[5] It is this very special world — one which led Talleyrand to declare that anyone who had not lived prior to the Revolution had no idea of the pleasures of life — that is at the heart of Gautier's play.

The curtain rises upon six men (a duke, four lesser noblemen, and one wealthy banker) calling upon a celebrated actress named Célinde. One of the men has paid for her house, another for the furniture. The others are rivals for the actress's favors. But she suddenly refuses them all. The reason, we learn, is that she has been reading Jean-Jacques Rousseau and now wishes to live a simple, rustic life. She is also influenced by a new lover, one Saint-Albin, who has convinced her of the joys of country living. So they leave Paris and go off to a hermitage (again like Rousseau) to live the idyllic life. Alas, there are toads on the floor, spiders in the beds, and wasps that fly in through the windows. Saint-Albin becomes bored with Célinde now that she refuses to wear jewelry or makeup and leaves her to marry a rich city girl. By the time the duke finally finds her, she is quite ready to return to Paris. The last scene shows her dethroning the actress who had taken her place and joyfully returning to the life of pleasure that she had once known.

The play is technically known as a *proverbe*, a play that takes some maxim and illustrates it in theatrical form. The genre goes back to the seventeenth century, but it was Alfred de Musset who made it famous, and several of his "proverbs" are still frequently played as curtain raisers to the main play at the Comédie Française. The proverb of Gautier's drama is "Bon sang ne peut mentir" ("Good blood will always tell"), which is the subtitle to the play as well as the closing line. This maxim is normally used in connection with an aristocrat who remains faithful to his honor, thanks to his fine "blood." Here it is used in ironic reference to Célinde, who, although not an aristocrat, comes back to her true milieu at the end of the play.

In its debunking of the beauties of the simple, rustic life, the play is obviously a facile satire of Rousseau. Despite the fact that he often longed to leave Paris for warmer climates, Gautier was nonetheless a man who loved the sophistication of the city. Nor would he have cared for Rousseau's moralizing. But *La Fausse Conversion* has another message as well, one that emerges from the lesson of the story. The play opens with an actress tired of a life in which she is bought, sold, and generally treated as a sex object. She is weary of the male attitude, so common among the aristocrats of the *ancien régime,* that a woman is a pleasure machine. So she gropes for something more authentic. Turning to the more serious Rousseau, she reads the *Social Contract* and seeks out a pure life in the country with a man she truly loves. Now the rhetoric of the play is that her new views are utter foolishness. Not only is the young man not pure, but she herself must inevitably weary of the "virtuous" life. Her nature (that "good blood" the proverb refers to) is to be an entertainer of men and a lover of her own vain pleasures. The men know this, and the play obliges her to recognize it as well. In short, *La Fausse Conversion* is another expression of Gautier's antifeminism. He cannot really accept a woman as a human being. She must, it seems, either be a source of pleasure for man or else frozen into an *objet d'art* like the Venus of Milo. Because of its didactic qualities, the play has little of the gratuitous fancifulness that Gautier wished to see in the theater. It is a competently constructed play but not one of Gautier's best.

III Le Tricorne enchanté

Le Tricorne enchanté ("The Magic Hat") was written or at least finished in early 1845. Perhaps because it contains no controversial ideas of any kind, Gautier risked having it performed. It was first staged at the Théâtre des Variétés on April 7, 1845. The plot, which sounds like one of Molière's, is age-old: Géronte, the old man, has a ward, Inez, whom he hopes to marry, but she loves the handsome, impecunious Valère. Thanks to the ruses of a wily servant, Frontin, and his female accomplice, Marinette, the old man is duped, the lovers are married, and the play ends happily.

The problem in a play of this kind is how to give originality to the hackneyed plot, and Gautier came up with an amusing idea. Géronte is fooled by being convinced that Frontin's old hat renders its wearer invisible. Thus he thinks he can overhear the "true" feelings of the young people. Inez and Valère are in on the deception, of course, and announce for his benefit that they are not in love with each other and that they both revere Géronte and wish to deed him their property. So they go off to a notary with the old man's permission and promptly marry.

But Gautier was not content just to vary the plot. We remember his desire to create a theater of fantasy. In *Le Tricorne enchanté* fantasy would come not only from the magic hat and the absurdities of plot it engendered but also from sheer verbal exuberance. In the opening scene, for example, Frontin runs into the equally unscrupulous Marinette. They joyfully trade insults, not that they are enemies, but merely to keep their repartee sharp. When Frontin then meets Valère and the young lover waxes lyrical, speaking of Inez's window as the heavens and describing dawn as smiling and rosy, Frontin punctures the young man's rhetoric with mocking rejoinders. The scene is but an excuse for verbal humor, since the dialogue in no way advances the action. Then Géronte gets into the act. When Frontin states metaphorically that his greasy old hat is his lodging, his wine cellar, and his kitchen (because when he is "invisible" he can steal bed, drink, and board), Géronte takes him literally:

> Il te sert de marmite!
> Je ne suis plus surpris alors qu'il soit si gras!
> Fait-il de bon bouillon?

(You use it as a pot? / I'm no longer surprised that it is so greasy! / Does it make good soup?)

Another scene shows Gautier's talent for verbal creativity at its fullest. Géronte has just fired his servant and wonders how to replace him. As he is a miser, the old man comes up with the idea of getting along without him altogether. This ordinary idea becomes transformed into the verbal concept of his being his own manservant. Thanks to the magic of words, he has suddenly become two people, and the idea explodes in a shower of fanciful wordplay. Géronte imagines himself being docile to his own commands, always obeying his master. As servant, he assures himself as master, that when paid he would hand the money back to his employer out of generosity. Should he be used by a suitor to pass letters back and forth to Inez, he could intercept them. In short, having created a double of his being through the chance of syntax and metaphor, he creates a whole fictional relationship between the two characters that springs to life for a moment through the magic of art. In *Le Tricorne enchanté* Gautier has added to the physical exuberance of farce an equal extravagance of language to create a truly charming play.

IV Pierrot Posthume

Gautier had already imitated the theatrical forms of the Middle Ages with *Une Larme du diable*, the seventeenth century with *Le Tricorne enchanté*, and the eighteenth century with *La Fausse Conversion*. His next effort was inspired by the tradition of the *commedia dell'arte*, which had entered France from Italy during the sixteenth century and had remained popular for at least two hundred years. Part of it has survived in modern times in pantomime, with Debureau its chief practitioner in the nineteenth century and Marcel Marceau today. In its standard version one finds three stock characters, Arlequin (Harlequin), Colombine, and Pierrot. Arlequin, dressed in many colors, is a blend of the credulous and the sly. Colombine was at first merely a servant girl, but then as the genre evolved, she became one of the lovers and usually eloped with Arlequin. Pierrot, a clownish figure dressed in loose white clothes and with whitened face, usually remained true to his role as a character out of pantomime and did not speak. He was greedy and without moral sense, but often in an innocent sort of way. Gautier took these characters, gave Pierrot the power of speech, added a quack doctor, and produced his own version of the age-old farce. As in the case of *Le Tricorne enchanté* verbal exuberance and physical horseplay are cleverly blended, but in *Pierrot posthume* ("Pierrot Back From the Dead") Gautier's inventiveness reaches its fullest expression.

Stripped of some of its secondary digressions, the plot is simple enough. Pierrot has been missing for some time, and the rumor is that he is dead. True, he had been captured by pirates and then hanged, but the rope broke and he escaped. Arlequin has persuaded his "widow," Colombine, to marry him just as Pierrot returns. Pierrot hears first Arlequin and then the doctor tell him that he is actually dead (Wasn't he hanged? Isn't he pale and white?), the former so that he may be free to marry Colombine, the latter so that he may sell the gullible Pierrot a quack "elixir of long life" to resurrect him. Pierrot at first believes them but finally learns the truth when his wife beats him to prove to him his own corporeality. The play ends with husband and wife reunited and Arlequin without a bride.

The plot, of course, is but pretext, as the opening scene makes clear. Arlequin offers Colombine a gift and asks her to guess what it is. She supposes it to be a ring, a watch, or diamonds, but it turns out to be a mouse in a cage. Why? So that Arlequin can make a speech in parody of seventeenth-century court preciosity:

> Cette pauvre souris, tournant dans cette boîte,
> Représente mon âme allant à gauche, à droite,
> S'agitant sans repos dans la captivité
> Où depuis si longtemps la tient votre beauté. (p. 169)

(This poor mouse, turning about in this box, / Represents my soul going from left to right, / Moving without rest in its captivity / Where your beauty has kept it for so long.)

The fantasy increases as the play progresses. When the Doctor offers Arlequin the secret family elixir, the latter suggests that all the doctor's ancestors must still be alive. The Doctor counters by creating a fantasy world of his own family:

> Nous ne pourrions jamais hériter de la sorte!
> Et, comme de la vie il faut que chacun sorte,
> Pour n'être pas contraints de nous assommer tous,
> C'est chose convenue et réglée entre nous:
> Aux vieillards, à cent ans, l'élixir se retranche,
> Et, comme des fruits mûrs, ils tombent de la branche. (p. 173)

(We could never inherit that way! / And as each must leave this life, / So that we won't have to bludgeon each other, / It is agreed among us all / That at the age of one hundred, the elixir is taken away from the old people, / And, like ripe fruit, they fall from the branch.)

This creation of a large family with its rather weird ethic has been conjured out of thin air by verbal play. It already suggests the technique that we saw in *Le Tricorne enchanté* when Géronte became his own servant. The technique reappears in identical form when Pierrot, convinced that he is dead, goes into mourning for himself. Like Géronte he is now two persons in one. He is so impressed by the fact that he has been so devoted to himself during life that he promises to attend his own funeral procession and then die of a broken heart on his own grave. This doubling of his own being leads to other zany scenes. There is one in which he decides to commit suicide, but this time "once and for all." In another the wild logic of the situation forces him to "remain dead" as Arlequin kisses his wife, because "a husband is cuckolded only when he is alive." To appear alive would result in a stain upon his honor and make poor

Colombine an adulteress. "I'm too moral for *that*," he concludes (p. 187).

The intensity of comedy increases if the effects can be cumulative. Just when all the gags seem exhausted and a resolution of the plot appears near, Gautier manages to spring one final surprise. Pierrot, now convinced by Colombine's beating that he is alive, turns on the Doctor and beats him. The idea is to prove that he is not dead, as the Doctor had claimed. The Doctor, ingenious to the end, having to admit Pierrot's corporeality, but still hoping to convince him that he is dead so that he can sell him his elixir of long life, pulls another verbal rabbit out of the hat by declaring, "You're a vampire" (p. 199). And once again the characters are off and running with this idea. Colombine is frightened lest Pierrot suck her blood; they all discuss possible "cures," such as a stake driven through the heart. And so it goes until the play staggers to its ritual happy ending. The spectator leaves the theater fully appreciative of the joys of a true piece of fantasy. Today's reader can only wish the play were performed more often, for it is one of the funniest brief comedies of the nineteenth century.

Théophile Gautier saw himself as a poet and a storyteller rather than as a dramatist. His attitude may perhaps be due to the simple fact that on the whole his talent for the theater was limited, but if he did not do more with drama, it may well be also because the times were not right. As we indicated at the beginning of this chapter, the theater of mid-century was dominated by dramatists and critics who insisted on conformity to conventional formulas acceptable to cautious middle-class audiences. As a consequence they were reluctant to welcome Gautier's experiments in verbal exuberance. Perhaps it was this climate of hostility to anything new that kept Gautier from developing his theatrical talent to its fullest and from becoming an important precursor of the imaginative theater of the twentieth century.

V *Ballets*

Romanticism brought a transformation not only to poetry and the theater but also to the ballet. As Gautier put it, the neoclassical decor of the past, "the twelve marble and gold mansions of the Olympians were relegated to the dust of storage bins" and were replaced by "romantic forests and glades illumined by the German moonlight of Henri Heine's ballads."[6] This change was highlighted in 1832 by the first of the great new ballets, *La Sylphide*, whose theme could not fail to delight any Romantic. The hero abandons his flesh and blood fiancée for an elusive sylph only to lose her as well and find himself totally bereft by the end of the ballet. The new era also ushered in the reign of the *prima ballerina.* Not until the twentieth century would the male dancer have more than a supporting role.

Another particularity of nineteenth-century ballet was that choreography was not paramount as it is today but secondary. Its function was rather to support the plot and the music. As a result the *prima ballerina* was not only the center of the dance, she was also the heroine of the story, and her acting ability and her beauty were as important as her technical virtuosity as a dancer. Ballet was often viewed as merely a special form of drama, and indeed there were efforts to adapt regular plays to ballets. Gautier was sophisticated enough to object to excesses of this kind. He wrote in 1846: "Ballet is a special genre, which requires subjects of a particular nature, in which the dance comes about inevitably, imperiously, and serves as the very expression of the story. A play translated into imitative gestures and accompanied by musical *divertissements* is not a ballet."[7] But even so Gautier could not appreciate ballet as pure motion. Despite his disclaimers he saw it as did so many of his contemporaries, as a kind of theater and as a series of beautiful poses.[8]

Indeed, Gautier came to the ballet through his admiration not for the dance but for the dancer, a fact that is not too surprising when one considers the importance of the *prima ballerina* and Gautier's love of feminine beauty. Writing of Taglioni, who danced *La Sylphide,* he commented, "Taglioni danced or rather floated a while in the air, with . . . soft abandon [and] voluptuously dying poses." He also observed that she had "leg movements and undulations of the arms that are worth an entire poem."[9] Gautier's passion for the feminine form was so great that he often wrote that he disliked watching male dancers.

If Gautier admired Taglioni, he fell in love with Fanny Elssler, the Viennese dancer who next became the rage of Paris. She was younger and prettier than her predecessor, and when she danced the Spanish cachucha (or cachuca), Gautier's enthusiasm knew no bounds. But she in turn eventually passed from the scene, and Carlotta Grisi became the talk of the town. The cousin of Giulia Grisi, the well-known opera singer, she was to be the dominant ballerina of the 1840's. Gautier, who had admired Giulia, fell in love with Carlotta, and although their relationship probably remained platonic, he never stopped loving her. In his later years he often visited her on her estate near Geneva in Switzerland. But if Carlotta rejected him as a lover, her sister Ernesta did not. She was the mother of Gautier's second and third children, Judith and Estelle. In fact, they lived almost maritally together for many years.

VI Giselle

Carlotta Grisi had made her debut at the Opéra in early 1841, dancing in *La Favorite*. She had been an immediate success, and Gautier had written on March 7 of that year: "She combines beauty, youth and talent — an admirable trinity."[10] It was for her that he wrote the world-famous ballet, *Giselle*. Anyone at all acquainted with ballet is familiar with this story of a girl who dies just before her marriage and becomes one of a group of elves, or willis, sinister woodland creatures who entrap any man who wanders into their domain. They force him to dance with them until he is exhausted, and then they topple him into a pond to drown.

On July 5, 1841, a week after the ballet's premiere, Gautier explained in the form of an open letter to Henri Heine in *La Presse* how he had come upon the idea for his ballet. "Leafing through your beautiful book *On Germany* a few weeks ago, I ran across . . . that passage in which you wrote about Elfs dressed in white dresses, whose hems are always a bit damp . . . Willis with their snowy features and their pitiless waltz . . . and I cried out despite myself — 'What a pretty ballet one could write with that!' In a fit of enthusiasm I even took a big sheet of white paper and wrote at the top . . . *The Willis, Ballet*. Then I began to laugh and threw the paper away, thinking that it would be impossible to put this misty nocturnal poetry on the stage."[11] At the opera that very evening, however, he met the librettist Vernoy de Saint-Georges, told him of his idea, and — according to his account — the libretto was completed in three days. Within a week Adolphe Adam had improvised the music and rehearsals were under way.

But the true story of the genesis of *Giselle* is more complicated than Gautier would have us believe, and besides, there are inaccuracies in his account, as Edwin Binney has shrewdly observed. Since the premiere of the ballet took place on June 28, 1841, one might assume that with such a whirlwind preparation the ballet's libretto must have been done in late May or early June. But the ballet was first announced on April 5, and the libretto probably dates from the end of March.[12] Various delays postponed opening night until late June. As for the music, Burgmüller contributed one piece, and both Coralli and Perrot had a hand in the choreography.

Furthermore, just how much of the libretto Gautier actually wrote has been a matter of intense scholarly debate. Gautier himself admitted that he didn't know how to kill off Giselle in Act I so that she could be a supernatural creature in Act II and that Saint-Georges had come up with the idea of having her die either of a broken heart or of a self-inflicted wound after learning that her supposedly stalwart rustic fiancé, Loys, is really a nobleman, Albert de Silésie, engaged to the beautiful Bathilde. For Act II Gautier had had the idea of presenting willis from different geographical regions. There would be French girls doing a minuet, German ones waltzing, but also oriental girls striking voluptuous poses. Fortunately, this idea was dropped before opening night, for a minuet and oriental dancing girls hardly seem suitable in a mysterious forest glade. Since the premiere, incidentally, other minor cuts have been made, with the result that today's production is more streamlined than the original.

These changes, plus Gautier's lack of experience as a librettist, have led critics to differing conclusions. Serge Lifar, Carlotta Grisi's biographer, assumes that Gautier merely had the original inspiration and that Saint-Georges was the real author.[13] The opposite view, again not totally convincing, is that Gautier did the entire libretto, for he always called it "his" ballet and claimed authorship for it. These critics also point out that Saint-Georges' other ballets seem to have a different style. Perhaps the most reasonable view is that Saint-Georges may well have written Act I, but it is almost certain that the second act is the work of Gautier.

Act II opens with Giselle rising from her grave (in 1841 wires were used so that the specters could actually soar through the air) to be initiated into the company of willis. Soon Wilfrid, the nobleman's squire, wanders into the clearing and is surrounded by spirits and whirled about until he is thrown into the water to drown. Then Albert, Giselle's unfaithful but remorseful lover, appears. He kneels by the cross of Giselle's tomb. The queen of the spirits orders Giselle to entice him away from the protecting cross so that he, too, will die. Obliged to do the queen's bidding, despite her reluctance, she does entice him away from his sanctuary, and he is about to follow Wilfrid into the pond when four o'clock strikes. It is the magical hour at which the willis must vanish until the following midnight, and Albert is saved. Bathilde, who had been looking for him, then appears, and he falls fainting into her arms as the curtain descends.

The motif of an alluring feminine sprite was of course not original.

It was at the heart of *Giselle's* precursor, *La Sylphide*, and in a larger sense could be found behind much of Romantic literature, for the sylph or willi is but a metaphor for the unattainable feminine ideal. But even if this motif was very much in the air during the 1820's and 1830's, it was not merely a convention for Gautier. As we have seen in previous chapters, it appears constantly in one form or another in his work and clearly reflects his own aspirations.

There is another motif appearing in Act II of *Giselle* that had often fascinated Gautier, the motif of the exhausting dance. Years before, he had been impressed by Hugo's poem, "Les Fantômes," whose heroine died from dancing to excess. In 1831 Gautier developed this idea further in his first short story, "La Cafetière" ("The Coffee Pot"). In this tale a young man goes to sleep in a strange room, and during the night characters step out of tapestries hanging on the wall and begin to dance in the room. The tempo accelerates until one of them, a beautiful young woman who had been warned that the dance could be fatal, collapses and dies of exhaustion. In *Giselle* the dance of death is transferred from the female to the male, with the result that the dangerous attractiveness of women emerges as a dominant idea and one that Gautier would develop further in some of his later stories. This particular motif of Romantic literature, the *femme fatale*, was one that would become the basis of the decadent movement of the latter half of the century.[14] *Giselle* was of its time, but it also prefigured the future.

Giselle became *the* ballet of the 1840's, just as *La Sylphide* had dominated the previous decade. Its very popularity showed that in 1841 the Romantic spirit was still very much alive, and its success was to inspire Gautier to write several more ballet librettos in the years that followed.

VII La Péri *and Other Ballets*

In 1843 Gautier composed another ballet for Carlotta Grisi. Entitled *La Péri* ("The Fairy"), it was inspired by one of Gautier's own short stories with an Arabian Night's flavor, "La Mille et deuxième nuit" ("The Thousand and Second Night"). Coralli was the choreographer, and the music was composed by Burgmüller. The story has nothing very new in it for anyone who knows Gautier. It is another dream of impossible love. The hero, Achmet, loves a fairy (or peri), and eventually the hero's death permits the two to be reunited beyond the grave at the ballet's end.

A few years passed before Gautier attempted any more ballets. In

1851 he composed the libretto for *Pâquerette* and in 1854 the one for *Gemma.* Neither ballet was a success, in part because they took too long to perform owing to numerous set changes. *Pâquerette* is set in France (Gautier's only ballet without some foreign, exotic setting) and recounts in comic fashion the trials of Pâquerette and a young village boy turned soldier. *Gemma* is a standard Gothic melodrama, complete with Italian setting and a villain who hypnotizes the heroine into docility. She is saved, of course, in the nick of time by the inevitable young hero. *Yanko le bandit,* whose premiere took place on April 22, 1858, was more popular than the previous two, but it adds little to our appreciation of Gautier as an artist. Set in Hungary, the ballet parades bandits, gypsies, and soldiers before the spectator's eyes. At the end the outcast hero dramatically abandons an irregular life and is accepted as an officer in the army. One has the vague feeling of watching a European version of Gilbert and Sullivan's *Pirates of Penzance* without the obvious parody of the English musical. *Yanko le bandit* need not be remembered.

Of interest primarily because of its setting, Gautier's last ballet, *Sacountala,* was first performed on July 14, 1858. The libretto is an adaptation of an ancient Hindu romance written by the poet Kalidasa. The ballet was a success not only because of its agreeable happy ending for the young lovers but especially because of the superb decor, consisting of the most luxuriant vegetation and of massive, brooding Indian palaces. The critic Edwin Binney does not hesitate to claim that the ballet did as much if not more than all the stuffy Orientalists and their learned articles to introduce Indian culture into France.

Today most critics of Théophile Gautier are usually little concerned with the later ballets. This indifference is no doubt due to the fact that all nineteenth-century ballets were based on a story and less exclusively on dancing, while the modern view is that plot is not of much importance. Since Gautier was responsible only for the story, modernists tend not to become very excited about his librettos, and it must be admitted that it is hard to take these obviously conventional plots seriously. But Gautier's ballets do show his continuing love for the exotic, and in *Giselle* he managed to combine the traditions of legend and romance with some originality in a libretto that is the basis for one of the world's masterpieces. It was an achievement of no small importance.

CHAPTER 6

Gautier the Storyteller

CRITICS of fiction have nearly always insisted that economy is the key to the successful short story. Edgar Allan Poe, for instance, stressed that the writer of short fiction seeks to achieve a single effect, and "he then invents such incidents, he then combines such events, and discusses them in such a tone as may best serve in establishing his preconceived effect. If his very first sentence tend not to the outbringing of this effect, then in his very first sentence he has committed a blunder. In the whole composition there should be no word written of which the tendency, direct or indirect, is not to the pre-established design."[1] The Russian formalist critic, B. Eichenbaum, who knew Poe's essay, made a similar distinction between long and short fiction and stressed Poe's idea that in the standard nineteenth-century short story the conclusion is the key to the tale.[2] Some of Guy de Maupassant's short stories provide the perfect model for a tale in which everything is directed toward the ending.

But Guy de Maupassant was not France's only important short story writer. Short fiction had in fact existed ever since the Middle Ages,[3] and by the first half of the nineteenth century the genre was becoming a major one, with writers as famous as Nodier, Mérimée, and Balzac contributing to its development. We saw in an earlier chapter that some of Gautier's earliest writing, *Les Jeunes-France*, consisted of short stories, and this youthful fiction was not just a passing fad with him. Short fiction, whether in the form of the *conte* (the short story) or the *nouvelle* (like the short story only longer), was to become one of his most important vehicles of artistic expression.

Gautier wrote so many stories that we have been obliged to choose only the best known or the most significant ones, for we cannot hope to deal with them all in a book of this limited length. Viewed as a whole, Gautier's *contes* and *nouvelles* fall roughly into two groups.

One consists of tales of the fantastic, the other of evocations of exotic Oriental splendor. We shall deal with the latter first. The Oriental stories all have a common inspiration: Gautier's desire to escape from daily reality into ancient cultures endowed with finer esthetic sensibilities and a greater degree of permanence than modern bourgeois France. Each of the individual stories, then, offers some variation of this quest for a distant ideal.

I "*Fortunio*"

Gautier's dream of inhabiting a tropical or Oriental paradise found one of its major literary expressions in "Fortunio" (1837).[4] Fortunio is a young Frenchman who has been brought up in the Far East by an incredibly wealthy relative who has indulged the boy's every whim. Having inherited his rich uncle's estate, he has returned to Paris when the story opens. With his vast wealth, perfect manners, and devastating handsomeness, he is the envy of the aristocratic social set. He is a loner, however, even if he is quite willing to be agreeable to those who know him. He remains unattached, and in fact none of his acquaintances (he really has no friends) knows where he lives. The plot is set in motion by his female counterpart, Musidora, an utterly ravishing courtesan bored by the limitations of the men she has known. She tries to conquer the elusive Fortunio and when she fails, initial irritation becomes hopeless passion. On the verge of committing suicide, she is saved by the arrival of Fortunio's carriage. He has learned of her interest in him and wishes to be courteous and gallant. Because Musidora's true passion now makes her more than coldly beautiful, Fortunio does reciprocate her love, and the two have an intense but brief affair. Fortunio cannot tolerate the idea of Musidora's having been possessed by others, however, even though now she loves him alone, for he is fierce in his desire for exclusive possession. He disappears and the broken-hearted heroine kills herself with a poisoned needle. Fortunio then returns to the East forever.

The plot summary gives little idea of the wild extravagance of the tale. Thanks to the hero's unlimited wealth, he is in a position whenever he entertains to buy a house, furnish it lavishly, and once the party is over, to sell the furnishings and disappear, leaving the empty house behind as a mute witness to his brief presence. In the heart of Paris Fortunio has secretly bought up an entire city block, glassed over the inner court, walled up the outside windows, and created an exotic paradise within. He calls it El Dorado, of course. Around the inner court marble stairs provide a graceful backdrop to orange and palm trees. Fortunio can order it to rain: invisible pipes, like a modern sprinkler system, shower pearl-like drops on the leaves of his virgin forest. Hummingbirds, peacocks, and birds of paradise add to the splendor with their color. Fortunio has brought not only his plants and birds but all his servants and the favorite girls from his harem, including a Javanese girl, Sondja-Sari, whom he loves as much or more than Musidora. None of the inhabitants of this Eden, we are told, have the slightest idea that they are in France.

Underlying all this nonsense there is seriousness of purpose. Fortunio is without question an idealized fantasy figure of Gautier himself. Gautier frequently imagined himself as a Turk with a harem, and when he heard Arabic spoken, he always felt that he knew the language but must have forgotten it temporarily. Further, the hero of the story, like his creator, is an excellent swimmer and very fond of cats. Ideologically, the two share a hostility for the doctrine of social progress and rail at the drab misery of wintry European capitals with their foul odors and dirt, and they both long for the autocratic rule and the lavish colors of the Orient. If Fortunio reflects Gautier, then through him Gautier is trying to work out an answer to an important human problem: How does one reconcile one's individual tastes and desires with the need for the presence of others? In the case of Fortunio others provide him with what he wants. Sondja-Sari and Musidora serve his pleasure and his self-esteem, and Fortunio very much wishes to keep these treasures to himself so that they can have no sense of independence. But in the case of Musidora even Fortunio with all his wealth is not omnipotent. He can burn down Musidora's house to destroy the gifts her admirers have given her but even he cannot decree that the memory of her past loves be abolished. His final flight from Western temporality to Eastern timelessness provides the logical conclusion to the plot. Time and memory, the only enemies Fortunio could not conquer, help affirm the independent existence of others and in doing so limit his power.

While shorter than novel length, "Fortunio," like many of Gautier's fictional pieces, is considerably longer than a short story. Whenever he was confronted with the chance to describe an exotic scene, Gautier could not resist the temptation to do so in great detail, with the result that he tended to write stories of intermediate length. Some critics have not liked his excessive descriptions.[5] Yet even with this "extra" length, the story is well constructed. The descriptions reinforce the themes and are therefore not superfluous but have the function of dramatizing an alternate vision to Western technology. All the details serve to move the story to its preordained conclusion. The conclusion, of course, is a familiar one — Fortunio-Gautier flees reality for a shimmering and unreal ideal.

II "*Le Roi Candaule*"

In "Fortunio" Gautier had built a wall separating East and West, thus making contact between the two impossible. In "Le Roi Candaule" (1844)[6] he did just the opposite. He located the action of his story in ancient Sardis in the Eastern portion of the Greek Empire, with the result that a clash between Western and Eastern cultures was almost inevitable.

The story of King Candaules goes back to Herodotus, although it is likely that Gautier became acquainted with it through a modern retelling, perhaps one of La Fontaine's *contes*. The story tells of King Candaules, who has married an Oriental princess named Nyssia. She is so beautiful that he would like his entire kingdom to admire her, but she has been brought up in the Asiatic tradition which cloisters women, and she refuses to go out without a veil or to reveal any part of her body to anyone but her husband. Unlike Fortunio, who insisted on keeping his treasures for himself, Candaules desperately wishes to share his knowledge of Nyssia's beauty with someone, so he chooses a close friend, Gygès, the Captain of the Guards, and obliges him to look upon his wife from a secret hiding place while she is disrobing for the night. Although reluctant, Gygès, who has been secretly in love with the queen for some time, is obliged to obey. At a critical moment Nyssia spots Gygès in his hiding place but pretends to notice nothing. The next day she forces Gygès to choose between instant death or murder. If he will kill the king, she will marry him so that it will remain true that no living man except her husband will have seen her body. Gygès chooses the latter course, kills Candaules while he sleeps, marries Nyssia, bribes the Delphic oracles to approve the match in order to quiet the restive populace. The story closes on this harmonious if slightly ironic note.

The meaning of the story is less easily discernible. At times the text seems to sympathize with Candaules' desire to show off his wife's beauty. Gautier presents the king as an art lover who would like to display Nyssia like a pearl that would shine in his diadem and be open to the "pure light of the sun," and when Gygès watches her disrobe, Gautier obviously seems to enjoy describing the strip tease over the captain's shoulder. Gautier even has a spotlight on her: "The light scattered around the bedchamber disdained to gleam off the golden urn, precious gems and the bronze pedestals and concentrated on Nyssia, leaving the other objects in the darkness" (p. 86). As Gygès has always been very respectful of the queen, one senses that the excited voyeurism belongs at least as much to the author as to the character.

In an attempt to raise the level of the story above voyeuristic titillation, Gautier tries to associate Candaules' desire to display the queen's charms to the frank openness of Western (Greek) culture, in contrast with the hermetically closed harem psychology of the East. The architecture reinforces the cultural dualism. Part of the palace is done in Greek style with delicate columns and open spaces, but the oldest part has great massive walls "of colossal proportions" (p. 69), reflecting the closed quality of ancient Oriental civilizations.

But in this tale of two cultures, the king's attitude is in fact not the dominant one. Instead, the text takes an attitude that Fortunio would have sanctioned. Let us view Nyssia first as a married woman. While she is a dutiful wife, she clearly does not love her husband. The reason is simple enough — her husband does not love her despite all his adulation. When he asks her to pose for him on a tiger skin, he sees her not as a person and not even as a sex object but rather as an *objet d'art,* and she makes it clear that she resents being dehumanized (p. 99). The text frequently mentions Candaules' pride in having such a treasure, but his pride is always self-serving. Further, her modesty is naturally outraged by her husband's exposing her to Gygès' eyes, and it is clear to her that her honor is being sacrificed to royal vanity. So she is not only willing to accept Gygès as her new husband, she even promises to love him, for she feels that Gygès truly loves her and would keep her for himself alone.

But Nyssia is more than a woman. We are told that she is made of an "ideal substance" (p. 61), that she is "divine" (p. 76) and "superhuman" (p. 82), and although married, she seems still to be an inaccessible virgin (p. 63). She is a kind of goddess, her divine form matched by divine power. While the legends whispered about among the citizenry that she has two pupils to each eye and that she can see through walls are only pieces of superstitious belief, she does in fact possess extraordinary vision that enables her to make out Gygès looking at her from his hiding place. Gods and goddesses are normally given acute vision, as the story of Acteon and Diana attests. This acuity of sight is a metaphor for the total knowledge that a god has of the universe over which he reigns.

If Nyssia is a kind of goddess, it is a natural corollary that like all divinities she is surrounded and protected by taboos. While the average citizen may worship from afar, only the true initiate may penetrate into her most intimate presence, and then only in adoration. Nyssia's divine decree is that only her husband may qualify for the ultimate revelation. Candaules fails Nyssia not only as husband but as worshiper. It is true that he is like a "priest intoxicated with the divinity who fills him" (p. 65), and he would like to "propagate her cult far and wide" (p. 67), but it is always his cult of beauty and not her divinity which interests him. Worse, to try to use a divinity to further one's own reputation and pride is sacrilege, and Candaules compounds his evil by forcing Gygès to violate his wife's sanctuary. For a mortal to violate a taboo means death, but Gygès is spared because he had not wanted to spy on Nyssia, considering it a "sacrilege" (p. 77), and because he accepts his inferiority to the goddess. There is a tradition in which Gygès has a ring which renders him invisible, but in this story he possesses no magic that might lift him above the merely human. Nyssia pardons him because he accepts his mortal status, and so it is Candaules who must die.

In fact, the rhetoric of the story more than suggests that "the gods" are behind all the action and that Nyssia's divinity is truly more than a metaphor. Pondering the remarkable series of events that would lead to his elevation to the kingship, Gygès wonders whether destiny had some "formidable reason" to unite the two (p. 77), and he believes himself to be aided by the gods (p. 78). He senses fatality pulling him along to his ultimate destiny (p. 104). There is some ambiguity here, for fatality is not presented as an objective truth by an omniscient author but merely as Gygès' own interpretation of events. But the concept of fatality is reinforced by a detail of the palace architecture. On one of the walls there are bas-reliefs of all of Candaules' ancestors arranged in a circle. The family line begins with Hercules and shows all the generations down to the king. Candaules' own likeness occupies the last place on the circle next to Hercules, leaving no room for any more. Gygès notes this detail and concludes: "The dynastic cycle is closed" (p. 70). Fate knows that Candaules will die without issue. The sense of fate communicated by this story is less overpowering than in Victor Hugo's *Notre-Dame de Paris* or in Gustave Flaubert's *Salammbô*, but it is clearly present. It must be understood in this connection that fate does not represent Gautier's personal explanation of existence but is merely an organizing principle for the story.

The conclusion, so important in shorter fiction, resolves the tensions between East and West, with the divinities of the East emerging as stronger than those of the West. The Greek Candaules has been murdered in the name of Oriental values, Gygès is incorporated into Nyssia's orbit, and even the Greek temples are manipulated with impunity, as shown by Gygès' bribe. Nyssia replaces Candaules as the major character and reigns triumphant as the incarnation of an Asiatic goddess with all her attendant taboos.

III "*Une Nuit de Cléopâtre*"

Théophile Gautier wrote two important stories whose action is set in ancient Egypt. "Une Nuit de Cléopâtre" ("One of Cleopatra's Nights"; 1838) was the first of these. It tells a story considerably less complex than "Le Roi Candaule." A young commoner named Méiamoün has fallen hopelessly in love from afar with beautiful Queen Cleopatra. He has always been a man who dared to face extreme danger. He would often go out hunting in the desert lightly armed and be gone for months. He had no fear of death. Indeed, "the abyss beckoned to him" (p. 18).[7] Eventually, eager to end the misery of loving in vain, he shoots an arrow with a note attached through a window of the queen's chambers. It reads: "I love you." As luck would have it, Cleopatra is bored and is intrigued by the mysterious note. Méiamoün next swims through an aqueduct into the queen's outdoor gardens and bathing pools where he is caught spying on her in her bath. As in "Le Roi Candaule" the penalty for this outrage must be death, but Cleopatra's vanity is flattered at finding a man who would so gladly throw away his life for her, so she proposes to entertain him lavishly for one night. At daybreak he will die. They feast sumptuously together, she dances erotically before him, and then as dawn breaks, Cleopatra is so touched by Méiamoün's courage that she is about to spare him so he may have the joy of loving her a little longer. But Marc Antony appears at that crucial moment, and Méiamoün says: "You see that the moment has come; it's the hour when beautiful dreams fly away" (p. 43). He drinks a deadly poison and dies. Cleopatra "sheds one burning tear, the only one she ever shed" and then lightheartedly turns toward Marc Antony. The story ends with her ironic explanation that the corpse on the floor is merely a slave on whom she was trying out a new poison.

The theme of impossible love is by now entirely familiar to our readers and need not detain us further. But the mythic substructure of the tale is worth closer scrutiny. Gautier first establishes the closed quality of his Egyptian universe. He points out that the blue of the Nile is doubled by the blue of the sky and that it is "difficult to decide whether the Nile reflected the sky or the sky reflected the Nile" (p. 5). One would expect that Gautier would then show the unity of this closed Egyptian universe as a fusion of the timeless male and female principles. The sun[8] and flooding Nile waters would combine to produce Egypt's agricultural fertility, and the divine family of Osiris, Isis, and their child Horus would reflect this climatic reality. But Gautier proceeded a bit differently, and it is this difference that gives the tale distinctiveness.

The Egyptian landscape is presented as totally desolate and sterile. "Nothing offset this aridity; no leafy oasis refreshed one's view; green seemed a color unknown to this nature; once in a while a palm tree spread its fronds against the horizon like a vegetal crab; a thorny cactus brandished its leaves as sharp as bronze swords" (p. 6). The sun is described in the same language of sterility that Gautier was to use in 1840 when describing the desolate regions south of Madrid for his *Voyage en Espagne:* "A harsh light, so intense that it was dazzling and dusty, poured out in torrents of flame, the blue of the sky turned white with the heat like metal in a smelting furnace; a blazing reddish haze smoked on the burned-out horizon. Not a cloud broke the uniformity of this sky, as unchanging and desolate as eternity" (p. 4). What is normally a life-giving male principle, the sun, becomes something "sinister" (p. 12), a principle of death.

Egyptian culture, too, is desolate. Instead of trees there are granite obelisks, instead of the good earth, granite paving and steps (p. 11). The living (of whom we see none, incidentally) seem to have "no other function than to bury the dead" (p. 5). This ancient world communicates a sense of total discouragement and seems to crush everything beneath its weight.

We find a strong contrast to the depressing landscape and burning sky, however, in the images of moon and water associated with the feminine principle of fertility. As the story opens, we see the queen in a magnificent boat shaped like a golden crescent moon gliding swiftly down the Nile. Her robe, so light that it seems woven out of air, undulates like a white vapor over her beautiful body. Feminine imagery is particularly evident in the description of Cleopatra's palace garden. Its luxurious coolness, its many pools and fountains, even its statuary all suggest feminine fecundity. Here is a good example: "At the end of the walk, one could find a large pool with four sets of porphyry stairs; through the transparency of the water which sparkled like diamonds, one could see the steps go down to the bottom which was sanded over with gold dust; from the breasts of women whose lower halves were encased in sheaths, spurted a perfumed water which fell back down into the pool in a silver spray" (p. 30). It is in this inviting area that the bored and dissatisfied Cleopatra waits for some fulfillment: "If I only had some passion, some interest in life," she complains, "if I loved someone or was loved . . . this arid and frowning Egypt would seem to me more charming than Greece, with its ivory, its temples of white marble, its copses of rose laurels, and its springs of living water" (p. 13).

Obviously, Méiamoün seems destined to fulfill Cleopatra's longing for a great passion. But one notes that their orgy stops short of sexual unity as if to suggest that Méiamoün cannot accomplish this desired goal. In fact, he is like the sterile climate he represents. He brings not creative love but a death wish. It is he who chooses to die as Marc Antony appears, for he is in love not with Cleopatra, or even with love, but with death. He is a precursor of all those sterile heroes of decadent fiction that populate so many works of literature, especially in the latter half of the nineteenth century. They all wish to die in a spasm of voluptuousness at the feet of some dominating, inaccessible woman. One may enjoy or be repelled by such a vision, but there is no doubt that in technical terms, Gautier's story is a success, for he harmonized his characters and his landscape perfectly. The ending, too, is well conceived. Its irony and detachment provide just the right tone for a story that celebrates the failure of human union.

"Une Nuit de Cléopâtre," like "Le Roi Candaule," emerges as an important story in the development of nineteenth-century fiction. It is well known, of course, that after 1835 prose fiction in France was moving away from Romantic medievalism in the direction of social Realism, but Gautier's stories point to another important direction that fiction was taking. Profiting from new discoveries in ancient cultures and religions, Gautier was wrestling with the problem of how to reconcile modern style and vision with the truths communicated by ancient mythic literature in a century dedicated to science and the doctrine of progress. By making his characters incarnations of opposing principles, he could have his human drama without abandoning a sense of the cosmic. Only Flaubert in *Salammbô* (1862) succeeded better than Gautier in recreating that mythic universe where the pre-Hellenic gods reigned supreme.

IV "*Le Roman de la momie*"

In contrast with his earlier Oriental stories, "Le Roman de la momie" (1857) is almost of novel length.[9] Indeed, Gautier may even have felt that his new story was a culmination of his efforts at writing fiction set in exotic lands. Certainly he lavished time and effort on it. His friend Ernest Feydeau had written *Histoire des usages funèbres et des sépultures des peuples anciens,*[10] and Gautier absorbed much of its contents. Openly avowing his debt to Feydeau, he studded his text with technical terms borrowed from his friend's scholarly study.

In "Le Roman de la momie" ("The Mummy's Tale") Gautier created a plot that had not one but a series of impossible loves. An ancient Pharaoh loves the princess Tahoser, but she in turn is in love with one of the Jews in bondage in Egypt. Unfortunately for her, he loves a Jewish girl. The Pharaoh dies pursuing the Jews through the Red Sea waters, and Tahoser, who becomes queen, dies shortly afterwards, apparently of a broken heart. The manuscript is her story.

Despite the fact that "Le Roman de la momie" is one of Gautier's best known titles, the work is in fact a very poor one. The defects of the story are multiple. The idea of describing the discovery of the manuscript was no doubt attractive to Gautier, but the consequences were awkward. The story must then be told not by an omniscient author but by an ancient Egyptian. Yet the main part of the narrative, purportedly written after Tahoser's death, indulges in endless pages of minute description. Not only are the descriptions without the symbolic function that they had in the two previous stories we examined, they are far too long. Nor would any ancient Egyptian feel the need to describe in such detail buildings and equipment that were totally familiar to him. As if this were not serious enough, the last part of the story, the Exodus, is a recreation *à la* Cecil B. De Mille. Curiously, the Biblical narrative with all its miracles is taken literally. The text, then, consists of three distinct parts: the discovery of the manuscript, the impossible loves of the Pharaoh and Tahoser, and the departure of the Israelites from Egypt. The three sections do not mesh well at all. While "Le Roman de la momie" does not enjoy a great reputation, its reputation is nonetheless overrated.

Gautier's Oriental tales are most successful when he keeps to the principle that Poe had enunciated — that short fiction must have great economy. "Le Roi Candaule" and "Une Nuit de Cléopâtre" are successful because every element has a clear function. Gautier's love of lush, exotic, even extravagant, description was always a danger for him, however, and made even the majority of his shorter tales longer than most short stories, and it positively ruined "Le Roman de la momie." Even so, Gautier made significant contributions to "Oriental" literature, and most of his non-Western tales are of high quality.

V "*Le Pied de momie*"

"Le Pied de momie" ("The Mummy's Foot"; 1840) really does not fit into Gautier's group of Eastern stories (even though a part of it takes place in ancient Egypt) because of the special nature of its plot. The narrator of the tale finds a mummified foot for sale in a Paris antique shop, buys it, and takes it home for a paperweight. That night he has a peculiar experience. He dreams that the owner of the foot, a beautiful Egyptian princess named Hermonthis, comes back from the past to claim it, but the foot, which now belongs to the narrator, will not cooperate until the new owner tells the girl she can have it back. To reward the hero for his generosity, Hermonthis gives him a green figurine from around her neck which will serve to replace the paperweight and then takes him back through time and space to ancient Egypt. There he meets her father. Now the reader has every reason to assume that this experience is but a dream. The text says so, and there is a lighthearted quality to the whole experience which suggests that it is not to be taken too seriously. When asked, for instance, by her father, the Pharaoh, what reward he would like for helping his daughter, the hero asks for Hermonthis' hand in marriage and adds: "A hand for a foot struck me as an antithetical reward which was in rather good taste."[11] But the young Frenchman is told that modern man lacks the durability of the ancient races and that he does not qualify. At this point the dream is interrupted by a friend who enters the narrator's room. All this is simple enough. But when the hero discovers in the place of the mummy's foot the little green figurine that Hermonthis left him, he is troubled. Was his dream a dream after all, or did something supernatural really happen during the night? The unusual ending of this story serves as a convenient transition from the first group of Gautier's shorter pieces of fiction, the Oriental tales, to the second group, his tales of the fantastic.

VI *Literature of the Fantastic*

There have been many efforts to define the "fantastic" in literature, so many in fact that some critics have despaired and concluded that any attempt to define the phenomenon is doomed to failure. Mathieu Galey calls it a genre which is "particularly resistant to any analysis or definition."[12] Yet to continue to use the term without defining it seems equally unsatisfactory. One might start with the idea that any violation of natural law, any appearance of the supernatural might constitute the fantastic, but this approach is no more useful than to define the pastoral as any work of literature which has sheep in it. Clearly, something is wrong with the idea of calling "Hark, the Herald Angels Sing" fantastic literature. The world revealed to us in Christmas carols is too joyous, and besides the angels are part of a coherent cosmic scheme. Modern man prefers to sense in the fantastic some element of fear, and H. P. Lovecraft concludes that fear is necessary for the fantastic to exist.[13] The idea behind the sense of fear or terror is that the character — and through him the reader — suddenly discovers that what he thought was an orderly, rational world is breaking down and that he can no longer control the rules of the game.

Another common criterion of the fantastic is the presence of uncertainty as to what is happening in the story. Hubert Juin in "Les Chemins du fantastique francais" talks about the triumph of uncertainty in the fantastic fiction of Cazotte, Nodier, and Nerval,[14] while Tzvetan Todorov uses the word "hesitation." In Todorov's eyes, if what seems to be a weird, supernatural phenomenon turns out to have a rational explanation, it becomes merely "strange," as in the plots of Ann Radcliffe's Gothic novels.[15] But should we learn for certain that the supernatural is "real" within the context of the story, Todorov ceases to call it fantastic and uses the label "le merveilleux," or the marvelous, so that for him it is fantastic only so long as we cannot be sure what we are dealing with.[16] This definition results in the fantastic's disappearing toward the end of most such stories, for we usually learn one way or another whether the supernatural is real. Todorov's attitude is perhaps overly restrictive, and we would prefer

Roger Caillois' definition. In *Au Coeur du fantastique* Caillois defines the fantastic as "a break in the recognized order of things, the eruption of the unacceptable in the midst of the unchanging daily legality."[17] The majority of all the definitions have much in common: the sudden sense of doubt about reality, the awareness of the presence of the supernatural, and the feeling of fear that accompanies our recognition of these phenomena, which forces radical reevaluation of our understanding of the nature of reality.

In historical terms, modern fantastic literature was a protest against an overly rationalistic view of man. In the eighteenth century interest in illuminism and the occult had flowered at the same time that the Enlightenment had tried to claim that man was an entirely knowable machine, activated and explained by the manipulation of his senses. It is no coincidence that Cazotte, the first of the modern writers of the fantastic, wrote during this period. The Romantics, too, felt that rationalism was dessicating, and they tried to enrich our understanding of man's nature by showing the importance of the processes of the unconscious, with the result that irrationality and dream played an important role in their art. Dreams often express dissatisfaction with daily reality and a desire to reach for something more agreeable that lies beyond it. But man has fears as well as desires, so that nightmare and hallucination form an inevitable part of any picture of the irrational. Dream literature, then, being a projection of both fear and desire is closely linked to evil, sin, and the forbidden, so that it often develops a strong erotic content.[18] The fantastic is achieved by concretizing the dreams enough to make them "real" in terms of the plot.

Gautier's own psychology explains in part his interest in the fantastic. All his biographers report that he was very superstitious and that he actually believed in the evil eye. He wrote a story about it entitled "Jettatura" (1857)[19] in which a young man, cursed with the *malocchio*, causes the death of his fiancée by looking at her too much. But psychology alone does not explain Gautier's fascination. Tales of the fantastic had become an important genre during the first half of the century, and Gautier was without question influenced by the popularity of this new literary tradition. In 1821 Charles Nodier had published "Smarra ou les démons de la nuit," which featured a wild midnight ride through a nightmarish landscape, and the following year he published "Trilby," whose plot revolved around the troubles of a Scottish family with a supernatural imp. Both stories appealed to the young Romantic generation, eager to reject an overly rationalistic view of man. Across the Rhine E. T. A. Hoffmann had been writing fantastic tales, and in 1830 his stories were translated into French and gave great impetus to the development of the genre. In that very year Gautier wrote an unpublished article praising the German writer.[20] "Onuphrius," which we examined earlier from a somewhat different point of view, owes much to Hoffmann, and a minor short story, "Deux acteurs pour un rôle" (1841) could almost be a translation from the German. Nor was Gautier alone among the major writers of his generation in cultivating the genre. Balzac and Hugo both explored its possibilities, and Prosper Mérimée's "La Vénus d'Ille" (1837) is one of the classics of the genre. Meanwhile, across the Atlantic Edgar Allan Poe and Washington Irving had begun to create an American version of this fascinating tradition.

VII "*La Cafetière*" and "*Omphale*"

"La Cafetière" ("The Coffee Pot"; 1831) was Gautier's first fantastic story. We summarized it in Chapter 5 in connection with the ballet *Giselle,* so it need not detain us much here. It is appropriate to point out that, although the hero's mysterious dancing partner dies, the reader feels little sense of terror, even though the narrator says that he was so terrified that his hair stood on end (p. 13). There are several reasons for the absence of any fear. First, the characters that emerge from the walls are entirely familiar and classifiable, being phantoms who have stepped out of eighteenth-century portraits. Another reason for the reader's serenity is that although the furniture (including the coffee pot) magically cooperates with the lively ghosts and takes on a life of its own, there is never any danger to the narrator. Bizarre as they may be, these events would not frighten the most susceptible reader. Finally, there is the strong possibility that the whole sequence of events never took place except in the narrator's dream.

"Omphale" (1834) is very similar to "La Cafetière." Again a young man is alone during the night. He informs us that while in bed he had a dream, "if it really was a dream" (p. 70). On the wall is an eighteenth-century tapestry representing Hercules and Omphale. The lady magically steps out of the cloth and explains that she is the Marquise de T*** who had posed for the tapestry. Over a series of nights she initiates the young man into the delights of sex and then with each dawn steps back into the wall hangings. The tone up to this point is lightly erotic and becomes gently comic when the boy's uncle suspects what is going on, for apparently the marquise had visited other men in that room. He grumbles, "That Marquise de T*** is really mad; where in the devil did she get the idea of falling for a snotty kid like him? . . . She promised she'd be good" (pp. 74 - 75), and he orders the tapestry rolled up and put away in the attic. At the story's end some years have passed, and the young man stumbles upon the tapestry in an antique shop. The lady seems to smile at him from the cloth, but before he can buy it, someone else makes off with it, and it is gone forever. But in an ironic thought at the end, the narrator decides that it is probably just as well, for one should not return to one's first love, and besides, "I am no longer young enough or handsome enough for a tapestry to come down off the wall in my honor" (p. 76).

There is little seriousness of tone in these early tales. It was as if Gautier had discovered a genre, was trying his hand at it, but did not really know how to take advantage of its possibilities for exploring the unknown. In "La Morte amoureuse" he opened up a more interesting perspective.

VIII "*La Morte amoureuse*"

"La Morte amoureuse" (1836) is a title hard to translate. "The Dead Woman in Love" is clumsy; "Love from the Grave" does not show gender; "The Succubus" or "The Vampire" are too limiting and suggest evil, which is not quite true. But whatever the title, the story is an intriguing one and probably the most widely known of Gautier's fantastic tales.

The story is told in the first person by an old Italian priest, Romuald, who recounts an extraordinary experience of his youth. This very form of narration creates an element of hesitation or doubt. Is the priest a reliable narrator? His sincerity seems beyond question, but even he is not certain what happened: "I still haven't figured out what was real and what was illusory" (p. 109). In any event, he tells of having been a young man innocent of any sexual experiences and about to be ordained a priest. At the ceremony he suddenly noticed a very beautiful woman in the church who made clear by her glances that she wanted him to leave the priesthood and become her lover. Although more than receptive to the idea and feeling indeed that a whole new wonderful world was opening up before him, he finds himself unable to stop the ceremony. He utters the fateful words that make him a priest forever. As he leaves the church a hand "as cold as the skin of a snake" (p. 86), yet which seems to brand him like a hot iron, touches him, and she says, "Wretch! What have you done?" A few moments later he receives a mysterious note: "Clarimonde at the Concini Palace." It turns out that Clarimonde is a notorious courtesan.

At this point the reader stops to ask himself several questions. Has the old priest wittingly or unwittingly deformed the real events of a half-century earlier? Even if he has not, problems remain. Is Clarimonde a live courtesan or a specter of some kind? Is she diabolical, as the cold burning touch would suggest, or does she represent life and love, as the young priest seems to feel (p. 84)? Romuald was aware of the uncertainty as he concluded, "I do not know whether the fire in her eyes came from Heaven or Hell, but it certainly came from one or the other. The woman was an angel or a demon or perhaps both" (p. 82).

Another priest, Father Sérapion, senses (no explanation is given as to how he learned about it) that Romuald is beset by some temptation and warns him against listening to the devil, but one is uncertain whether to assume Father Sérapion's point of view, even though he announces that dreadful things go on at the Concini palace.

At this juncture Romuald leaves for another town and settles into his clerical duties. One night he thinks he sees a mysterious woman lurking in his garden among the trees. He can find no one and wonders if it was an illusion. Some nights later a mysterious man calls him away to a deathbed. A wild nightmarish ride of obviously diabolical nature leads to a home with a woman lying dead on a couch. It is Clarimonde. Romuald kisses her, and she responds to his kiss, saying, "I've waited so long for you that I died. But now we are engaged and I can see you and visit you. Farewell, Romuald, farewell! I love you; that's all I wanted to tell you and I give you back the life that you gave to me for a minute with your kiss" (p. 99). The priest is so overcome that he faints.

When he revives, he is back in his house, and his servant confirms that the experience was not a figment of his imagination, for she saw the mysterious man bringing Romuald home. In fantastic literature it is necessary to establish the sense of reality — Caillois' "daily legality" — in order for the sense of the fantastic to have much effect. The servant's testimony heightens the reader's apprehension. Then Father Sérapion arrives to inform the younger man that Clarimonde died the previous night after a week-long orgy, and he suggests further mysteries when he says cryptically, "They say it isn't the first time she has died" (p. 102).

In the last part of the story Romuald leads the life of an average priest during the day, but at night he dreams with such vividness and precision that he cannot be sure whether the nocturnal experiences are not the true reality and the daytime life the illusion. At night he becomes a handsome young nobleman and the lover of Clarimonde. Their life together is delightful, but Clarimonde begins to weaken and look pale. By chance she sucks Romuald's blood when he cuts his finger, and the color comes back to her cheeks. She realizes that she is a vampire and needs blood to survive. So, periodically she drugs her lover to take a little of his blood. Suspicious, Romuald avoids the drug one night and discovers the truth. But he is touched by the fact that Clarimonde is very gentle and considerate. She takes only enough to restore her health but not enough to hurt him.

Father Sérapion comes to suspect the truth and urges Romuald to accompany him to open Clarimonde's grave. Romuald agrees: "I was so tired of this double life. . . . I wanted to know once and for all whether it was the priest or the gentleman who was the victim of an illusion; I was determined to kill off one or even both of the two, for this life could not go on" (p. 114). When the grave is opened, they find her lying there in all her beauty. Father Sérapion sprinkles holy water on her and she crumbles away. That night she makes one last visit to Romuald to tell him that now she must leave him forever, and she does. Romuald ends the story by saying that he regrets achieving "peace of soul" (p. 117) at such a cost. A final unconvincing moral (no doubt appended to satisfy the censors) warns against looking at women, for, it claims, one's salvation is at stake.

All fantastic literature tends to have some kind of meaning. Much modern science fiction (often a type of fantastic literature) is only thinly disguised social or political rhetoric. In the nineteenth century the events that take place in fantastic literature are more often metaphors for psychological truths which a pre-Freudian era did not dare admit openly. As a case in point, Tzvetan Todorov believes that Romuald's kissing Clarimonde on her deathbed is a disguised expression of necrophilia.[21] But this interpretation is based on the idea that Clarimonde represents something evil as well as desirable. In fact, the story is much more ambiguous than this. Not only is reality unclear at times, the moral values are far from simple. Sérapion is "good" and Clarimonde "evil" only up to a point. Underneath the surface story one notes that Sérapion is harsh, suspicious, and domineering, whereas Clarimonde is considerate and loving. Viewed in this light, Romuald's kiss is far from evil and can be incorporated into the fairy tale traditions of Snow White and Sleeping Beauty, where kisses are life-giving. Even Clarimonde's vampirism is not necessarily evil. Having drunk her lover's blood, she exclaims in rapture, "[Now] my life lies in your own, and everything that is me comes from you" (p. 111). The vampirism is a metaphor for total love. In short, "La Morte amoureuse" is asking: Is asceticism really more virtuous than ardent love? And the answer hesitates to the very end. This uncertainty, incidentally, causes what one might call a theological defect in the story. If Clarimonde is not wholly evil, she should not be annihilated by holy water. If she is evil, she should have revealed it in her actions, which she did not.

As a metaphor for the problem of personality, however, the story is clearer. The basic construct of the tale, the priest-nobleman antithesis, speaks once again to Gautier's concern with the problem of the split personality.[22] The narrator confesses that his nature "had, so to speak, become double" (p. 108), and the hesitation of the tale represents uncertainty concerning the dominant part of the two halves. In "La Morte amoureuse" ontological uncertainty is added to moral ambiguity. It is not only hard to know who one is but also who one ought to be.

IX "*Le Chevalier double*"

In 1840 Gautier wrote a short fantastic tale in which the basic idea of "La Morte amoureuse" is even more clearly visible. "Le Chevalier double" ("The Twin Knight") comes directly out of the tradition of the German *Doppelgänger*, Musset's "La Nuit de décembre," and on this side of the Atlantic, Poe's "William Wilson." The hero is a medieval knight whose father was the Devil and whose mother was a virtuous woman. As a result the child is born with a split personality. One day he is vicious, the next kind and considerate. To win the lady of his choice in marriage, he must eliminate his negative self. He does so in the most literal of terms. He meets his own mirror image on the field of battle and after a hard fight kills him. He then becomes a stable and virtuous man. In this story the issue is clear-cut, for there is no moral ambiguity to confuse the hero's choice, and the outcome is a happy one.

X "*Arria Marcella*" and "*Avatar*"

In "Arria Marcella" (1852) Gautier reverted to the ambiguity of "La Morte amoureuse." The hero is a young French tourist visiting the ruins of Pompeii. He sheds a tear at the spot where a beautiful young woman had died. He knows of her existence because he has examined a lava mold of her bust which has survived the centuries. That night the city comes to life as he wanders through it; the girl appears and announces that his tear brought her back to life. Later her father (a Christian), who is appalled by her cult of pagan beauty, anathematizes her, and she crumbles to dust. Again there is a contradiction in the idea behind the story. Human love of beauty brings Arria Marcella (the heroine) to life, but Christian asceticism destroys her. If it were not that the entire tale may be only a dream (the hero is awakened the next morning in the ruins), the coexistence of two opposing religions, each with full power over the natural order, would be clumsy indeed.

The desire to return to Pompeii and become a Roman is clearly a metaphor for the wish to become someone else. But Gautier knew perfectly well that it is impossible to become another individual, and he expressed his belief forcefully in one of his most curious stories, "Avatar" (1857). The title is used, not in its strict Hindu sense of the incarnation of a deity, but in its looser meaning of the transformation of one person into another. Gautier sets up an interesting plot. Octave de Saville has been in love for some time with the Countess Prascovia Labinski. Unfortunately for Octave, the lady loves her husband, Olaf, passionately and will not overstep the bounds of friendship with the young Frenchman. Octave is slowly dying of unrequited love. The plot is set in motion by the arrival of a Doctor Cherbonneau who has learned the mystic secrets of the East and especially how to summon a soul (in the form of a blueish electric spark) out of the body. To solve Octave's problem, he lures Count Labinski to his studio and when both he and Octave are unconscious swaps their two souls. Octave awakens with Labinski's body (and vice versa) and is now in a position to become the Countess' lover thanks to a perfect disguise. This attempt to play the role of Amphitryon fails, however, for the message of the story is that a person is not defined merely by outward appearance. The Countess is uneasy in her "husband's" presence and closes her door to him until he can speak endearingly to her in Polish. So Octave gives up and permits the doctor to give Labinski (furious at being trapped in Octave's body) back his soul. The old doctor, whose body is worn out, moves his soul into Octave's young body, and Octave gladly accepts death. His soul is last seen disappearing out the window and soaring up into the sky.

Gautier, like the Goncourts, has often been accused of attributing value to exterior surfaces and forms alone. The perfectly preserved female figures from the past (Tahoser's mummified body in "Le Roman de la momie" and the mold of Arria Marcella in the story of that name) have lent credence to this view. But Gautier was after all a real person in contact with real people, and it is obvious that by 1857 he had had a great deal of experience in living. His trip to Spain, his many friends, the women whom he had loved and who had loved him in return, and the three children whom he had fathered, all contributed to his appreciation of the complexities of human life. By now he knew emotionally what he must have always known intellectually, that there is a difference between the human personality with all its complexity and erotic fantasy with its dehumanizing reduction of an individual to an idealized sex object.

XI "*Spirite*"

In the eyes of many critics "Spirite" (1865) marks the culmination of Théophile Gautier's efforts to express his vision of the world in artistic terms, and it is widely considered to be the most lyrical, sensitive, and important of his fantastic tales. Marc Eigeldinger, in his introduction to the most recent edition of the work, believes it to be, in spite of its fantastic qualities, "the transposition of autobiographical elements and . . . [the] expression of a spiritual plan."[23] Albert Smith is convinced that it marks the final stage of an evolution in Gautier away from an attachment to the material to a more spiritualized vision.[24]

There can be no doubt that "Spirite" was important to its author. If Gautier lived maritally for twenty years with Ernesta Grisi and if he had a brief, passionate interlude with Marie Mattéi from 1849 to 1852, he never let other attachments divert his love from his idol, Carlotta Grisi. It was on her estate that he wrote much of "Spirite," and it was for her that he wrote it. In November, 1865, he sent her an inscribed copy in which he urged her to read, "or rather reread, for you know it already, this poor tale which has no other merit than to reflect [your] pleasing image, to have been dreamed under your large chestnut trees and perhaps written with a pen that your beloved hand had touched. . . . The idea that your charming eyes will be fixed for a time on these lines where, under the veil of fiction, the true, the only love of my heart is palpitating, will be the sweetest reward for my labor."[25] Gautier was proud of the final result and believed that "Spirite" contained some of the finest pages that he had ever written.

The hero of the story is Guy de Malivert who, not surprisingly, has many of Gautier's own character traits and who has lived partly as Gautier actually did and partly as Gautier would have liked to live. He is a bachelor who enjoys living alone and reading by a warm fireside on a cold winter's evening. Like Gautier, he likes cats, a good cigar, and beautiful women (probably in that order). He has traveled to Spain, Italy, Germany and Russia. In art, Malivert admires the Acropolis as much as Gautier did, and they both take pleasure in composing sonnets to fit a preconceived rhyme scheme. If both enjoy pretty women, both are also afraid of marriage. Unlike Gautier in 1865, however, Malivert is extremely rich and in the prime of life, whereas Gautier was limited financially and his growing corpulence and weakening heart made it impossible for him to play the role of the dashing lover.

The story opens as Malivert is on the point of drifting into marriage with a highly eligible widow, Mme d'Ymbercourt. He begins to get the feeling that some emanation is around him, and indeed, strange things begin to happen. He discovers that he has written a rude letter to Mme d'Ymbercourt that breaks off their relationship when he had not consciously intended to; then he hears an inexplicable sigh. Malivert has a friend, Baron Féroë, a Swedish diplomat, who is an initiate of Swedenborgian mysticism. He announces to the bewildered hero that the spirit world has its eyes on him and that he should make no earthly attachments. Little by little the spirit world (or the ideal) overcomes what little attachment Guy de Malivert has for the real, and finally a beautiful girl materializes for the hero in the depths of his Venetian mirror. She communicates with Guy by means of dictation through his pen when he is in a trance. Her story — a lengthy part of the narrative — explains that she had loved Guy when on earth but he had never seen her and she had died in a convent. By special dispensation (from whom is not made quite clear) she has the right to return to make herself known to him. Guy falls in love with her and almost commits suicide to join her but is warned just in time that suicide would separate them forever. Fortunately, he is killed by bandits while on a trip to Greece, and the two lovers are reunited in Heaven. Baron Féroë in a final ecstatic vision sees "in the middle of an outpouring of light that seemed to come from the depths of eternity, two bits of light of even greater intensity, like diamonds in a flame, twinkling, palpitating and coming together, taking on the form of Malivert and Spirite. They flew near each other in a celestial and radiant light, caressing each other with the tips of their wings . . . and finally like two drops of dew on the same leaf, blended into a single pearl" (p. 215).

"Spirite" quickly became popular among believers in Swedenborgian mysticism. Emile Bergerat says that Gautier received innumerable letters from initiates who talked to him "as if he were a priest of this bizarre religion."[26] But it would be a mistake to make any facile assumption that Gautier was himself a believer. "Le Roi Candaule" was organized around the concept of Oriental fatality, but as we suggested earlier, we need not presume any special adherence on Gautier's part to a doctrine of fatalism. "Le Roman de la momie" presents the Judaic version of the miracles in Egypt as "true." In "La Morte amoureuse" and "Arria Marcella" Christian exorcisms and anathema reduce apparently diabolical creatures to dust, yet it would be folly to assume that Gautier, who was often anti-Semitic and anti-Christian, believed personally in the religion of his stories. In fact, Gautier warned within "Spirite" itself that one should not believe everything an author says: "One must allow for literary or philosophical systems or other fads of the moment, [as well as] for what the author cannot say, the style that has been chosen or imposed, . . . literary imitations — everything that can modify the writer's exterior forms" (p. 117). Metaphysics in Gautier's fiction serves an esthetic rather than a religious or metaphysical function, providing a coherent and attractive framework for the story and imparting the tonality that Gautier wished it to have. In the case of "Spirite" Gautier may also have wished it all to be true, but that is as far as one dare venture safely. To exaggerate Gautier's evolution toward metaphysical idealism is dangerous. The most we can say with assurance is that the disengagement from the interests of the real world that is so clear a motif in "Spirite" is a reflection of Gautier's fatigue. Now in his midfifties, he was unconsciously preparing himself for death.

Viewed as a fantastic tale, "Spirite" soon loses any sense of hesitation in the sense that Todorov stipulates. Nor does it have Lovecraft's sense of fear, for once Spirite makes a definite appearance, we learn that she is entirely beneficent. The point of the tale lies not in its "fantastic" qualities but elsewhere, and as one might surmise from the plot summary, it deals — once again — with Gautier's real-ideal dichotomy. At one period in the story the narrator remarks ironically that there is a limit to everything, even to a conversation on the real and the ideal, yet the text belies this assertion. Guy has lost interest in the social whirl and in his daily life, so when the ideal world is opened up for him by Spirite and Baron Féroë, he is enchanted. But what is of special interest here is that Malivert-Gautier expresses the concept of the ideal as something attainable, not in life, but in art.

> The next day [after seeing Spirite in the mirror] he sat down to work. His enthusiasm, which had been dormant for a long time, was rekindled, and ideas crowded into his brain. Unlimited horizons, endless vistas opened before his eyes. A world of new feelings fermented in his chest, and to express them he asked of language more than it could give. The old forms, the old molds burst. . . . Never had he risen to such a height, and the greatest poets would have signed what he wrote that day. (p. 177)

Spirite agrees with Guy's own judgment: "Genius," she remarks, "is truly divine. It invents the ideal, it glimpses higher beauty and the eternal light" (p. 178). In short, the whole tale of "Spirite" is more than a metaphor for Gautier's wish to rejoin Carlotta Grisi beyond the grave.

That the effort of creating a work of art could be full of danger was recognized by many different writers of the nineteenth century. Balzac's "Le Chef-d'oeuvre inconnu" and Zola's "L'Oeuvre" are both stories of painters who lose their reason in an attempt to paint the perfect painting. As we saw earlier, Gautier had understood as early as 1832 when he wrote "Onuphrius" the danger of losing contact with the real. Spirite warns Guy that there is danger ahead for him: "This invisible world, veiled by reality, has its traps and its abysses" (p. 109). Later her language resembles that of Victor Hugo, the visionary. Describing the universe that she had discovered after her death, she tells Guy: "The Milky Way streamed across the sky like a river of molten suns. The stars that I now saw in their true form and grandeur [were] shining with immense wild flames. Behind them . . . in ever more dizzying depths, I could see others and still others so that the depths of the firmament were nowhere visible" (p. 161). The vertigo of the infinite threatens every great artist, but even if the writer retains his balance, the completion of the perfect work of art, Gautier believes, is not of this world. The paradox of the artist is, of course, that the greater he is, the greater his sense of dissatisfaction with what he can achieve with his finite means. From "La Cafetière" to "Spirite" (despite the success of the early "La Morte amoureuse" and the failure of the later "Le Roman de la momie") there is a general maturing of Gautier's talent, and it was when his style reached its culmination and when he succeeded the best that he was most aware of his imperfections.

XII *Gautier and the Artificial Paradises*

Frequently included among Gautier's fantastic stories are two in which he tells of taking opium and hashish. The effect of the drugs created an "artificial paradise" (to use an expression popular at the time) as the orderly processes of reason broke down and weird and fantastic shapes and scenes haunted the mind. The first of these, "La Pipe d'opium" (1838), tells of a visit to his friend, Alphonse Karr, who offers him some opium. That night Gautier relives in a narcotic dream his morning visit to his friend. His experience (in the dream) starts with no deformation of reality, but soon objects dissolve or become transparent, and all around him "networks of fire and torrents of magnetic emanations fluttered and whirled, weaving together and closing in ever more inextricably. Dazzling threads of light came up to each of my pores and implanted themselves in my skin like hairs on one's head" (p. 125). Then a semblance of a plot unfolds. A carriage appears at the door, and soon the narrator is off on a wild ride across a sinister landscape. He arrives at a strange house where he finds a dead woman whom he kisses. She responds avidly. Then the continuity of the dream is broken. In a different home a mysterious woman who is the dead person he had kissed calls upon him. He knows her name is Carlotta, that she had died young, and that she missed the pleasures of this world. The dream begins to become erotic, but it and the story end with Gautier's cat waking him up.

The other drug-inspired vision, "Le Club des hachichins" (1846), is somewhat similar, although lacking the erotic content of the first one. The story takes place in the Hôtel Pimodan on the Ile Saint-Louis in Paris, a residence famous because Charles Baudelaire lived there. In his monograph on Baudelaire Gautier states that he did not meet the author of *Les Fleurs du mal* until 1849, but there is every likelihood that this date is in error and that they had become acquainted a few years earlier. At any rate, by 1846 many French artists had had considerable experience with drugs. If Balzac had refused to touch drugs because they might weaken his sense of will, Gautier and Baudelaire were less cautious, but neither of them let drugs dominate them. In his "Poème du hachich" Baudelaire warns artists that drugs destroy the will and one's critical faculties. Gautier was careful not to take drugs more than a few times in his life. He had had his first experience with hashish in 1843, and in "Le Club des hachichins" he records an evening spent with others taking that drug.

These experiences with drugs, whatever their interest, do not truly qualify as tales of the fantastic. There is no hesitation, no supernatural, no fear. We know from the beginning that the hallucinatory world is not real but a product of chemically distorted senses. Even the descriptions are lucid accounts of hallucinations. The syntax and the vocabulary are under total control as Gautier tries to convey after the fact the nature of his experience.

But if the stories are not fantastic in any strict sense, they have nonetheless intrigued critics interested in Gautier's creative processes. Did Gautier make use of the visions he saw while under the influence of drugs to enrich his descriptions in other stories? As a case in point, Emanuel Mickel in *The Artificial Paradises in French Literature*[27] notes that in "Le Pied de momie" the little figurine that Hermonthis left behind was made of a green paste ("pâte verte") and that hashish is taken in the form of a green jam or paste. There is one passage in the story that reminds Professor Mickel of a drug-induced hallucination. While on his magical flight to ancient Egypt with the princess, the narrator has that "sense of timelessness which is so characteristic of the hashish experience,"[28] and Gautier's text refers to a "powdery mist" and a "fog of eternity" (p. 161). But caution is advisable here. Not only does Mickel place Gautier's first experience with hashish three years after the story was written, but it is almost impossible to guess the accuracy of Gautier's accounts of his own hallucinations. Both "La Pipe d'opium" and "Le Club des hachichins" were written to be published and read. How much did Gautier invent or borrow from other accounts (like De Quincey's) which in their turn may have been in part invented or copied? How much did Gautier falsify his narratives to make them more interesting or readable? At the end of his analysis of Gautier's work Professor Mickel admits that drugs seemed to have had little effect on Gautier's poetry, and he warns against any assumption that Gautier wrote descriptive prose passages while under the influence of intoxicants. He ends up by sharing our own suspicion that literary borrowings explain some of the so-called "hallucinatory" passages. But there remains the likelihood, as Mickel claims, that certain descriptions (certain passages in "Avatar" and "Spirite," for instance), while not exact reproductions of Gautier's visions, were nonetheless inspired by his drug experiences.

CHAPTER 7

Emaux et camées and Other Poems

I *Gautier's Vision of Art in* Emaux et camées

EMAUX *et camées* ("Enamels and Cameos") was Théophile Gautier's final volume of poetry and the one for which he is best known. Its first version, printed in 1852, contained only eighteen individual poems, to which over the years Gautier added twenty-nine, ending with the edition of 1872 compiled shortly before his death.

In his essay of 1867, "Rapport sur les progrès de la poésie," Gautier explained that his goal in writing *Emaux et camées* was "to treat small subjects in a restricted manner," and he compared his poems both to "the medallions that are inlaid into the covers of jewelry cases," and to miniatures etched in agate, cornelian, and onyx. Gautier considered the alexandrine with its twelve syllables "too vast for these modest goals, and . . . has used only octosyllabic verse, which he has melted down, polished, and chiseled with all the care that he could."[1]

If the volume is still remembered today, it is because historians of literature have found it an ideal expression of the doctrine of Art for Art's sake. The first and last poems of *Emaux et camées* contain the essence of the poet's attitude. The opening sonnet is entitled "Préface:"

> Pendant les guerres de l'Empire,
> Goethe, au bruit du canon brutal,
> Fit *le Divan occidental*,
> Fraîche oasis où l'art respire.
>
> Pour Nisami quittant Shakespeare,
> Il se parfuma de çantal,
> Et sur un mètre oriental,
> Nota le chant qu'Hudhud soupire.

Comme Goethe sur son divan
A Weimar s'isolait des choses
Et d'Hafiz effeuillait les roses,

Sans prendre garde à l'ouragan
Qui fouettait mes vitres fermées,
Moi, j'ai fait *Emaux et camées*.[2]

Obviously, Gautier had not changed since the days of "Fortunio" and "Le Roi Candaule." The West represents action, politics, temporality, and power. The poet is so hostile to his culture that he even rejects Shakespeare as being too *engagé*. The East is isolation, beauty, the song of a magic bird (Hudhud), and the poetry of Hafiz. Gautier has again chosen the delicate stasis of a Persian garden over the brute dynamism of the West.

The last poem of the collection, even more famous than the opening one, completes the idea of Art for Art's sake. Entitled "L'Art," it was published, most appropriately, in *L'Artiste* on September 13, 1857. Three key stanzas summarize the essentials of Gautier's thought:

Oui, l'oeuvre sort plus belle
D'une forme au travail
Rebelle,
Vers, marbre, onyx, émail.

Tout passe. — L'art robuste
Seul a l'éternité.
Le buste
Survit à la cité.

Sculpte, lime, cisèle;
Que ton rêve flottant
Se scelle
Dans le bloc résistant.[3]

The first and third strophes cited above suggest that painstaking craftsmanship and not Romantic inspiration creates art. The second indicates that, thus created, art can outlast society, an idea that Gautier had already incorporated into "Arria Marcella," where the lava bust of the heroine survived the fall of the Roman Empire.

It should be pointed out that Gautier did not always express his admiration of art and the artist in terms of durable stone or gems. In

"Variétés sur le carnaval de Venise" he shows art as beautiful but fragile. One poem from the group tells how an old tune butchered by a local fiddler, imprisoned by the bourgeois in their music boxes, and danced to by sweaty workers, can be transformed by a great artist. The poet imagines the immortal Paganini taking up the old melody "with the tip of his bow" and "embroidering its faded gauze, still red from its cheap tinsel," and by musical alchemy creating from it "arabesques of true gold."

But there is more to *Emaux et camées* than these poems about art suggest. Many others are in fact quite personal, frequently using the pronouns "I" and "me." "Le Château du souvenir" is openly biographical, and the poet reminisces about the wonderful moments of his youth. Many others are clearly inspired by his love for different women, so one might surmise that he is actually indulging in Romantic sentiment. But there is nonetheless a difference. In most cases these "personal" poems communicate little sense of intimacy, for the human experience is quickly immobilized into a "cameo." Nevertheless, many critics have enjoyed the volume because of these biographical elements. Joanna Richardson claims it to be "powerful and significant . . . because it enlightens many moments of Gautier's life."[4]

II *The Structure and Meaning of* Emaux et camées

Emaux et camées has more often been appreciated for the formal perfection of its verse. René Jasinski calls it "a miracle, with virtuoso craftsmanship [and] sureness of taste."[5] But biographical details and technical expertise have not satisfied most twentieth-century critics. Many readers have complained that there is no substance behind the form and that the poems are "empty." The criticism is overly harsh. Who could object to the delicate Mallarmean charm of the following strophe taken from "Fantaisies d'hiver" ("Winter Fantasy"):

> Dans le bassin des Tuileries,
> Le cygne s'est pris en nageant,
> Et les arbres, comme aux féeries,
> Sont en filigrane d'argent.

(In the Tuileries pools/The swan was frozen in as he swam/And the trees, as in the *féeries,*/Are filigrees of silver.)

Furthermore, these "limited" poems, if grouped properly, create a coherent vision of man's present reality and constant longing, providing the volume with a thematic unity and a "substance" that critics have said it did not have.

Gautier begins with a critique of the reality of man's existence in Paris. In the poet's eyes the weather in the capital is usually cold, gray, and cheerless. Greedy bourgeois rush madly about in pursuit of their perverse pleasures (Poem IX). As for working-class people, their pleasures do not rise above the level of Saturday night public dances with all their noise and sweat. Nor is there any hope of finding a perfect love in some isolated garret to compensate for the ugliness:

> Pour la grisette et pour l'artiste,
> Pour le veuf et pour le garçon,
> Une mansarde est toujours triste:
> Le grenier n'est beau qu'en chanson. ("La Mansarde")

(For the shop girl and for the artist,/For the widower and for the bachelor,/A garret is always sad:/Attics are gay only in songs. — "The Garret")

Gautier's reaction to this ugly reality is predictable. Like Fortunio, he seeks to escape it, and like Guy de Malivert of "Spirite," he can barricade himself by a warm fire with his books on a cold winter night (Poem XLVI), but even here winter (= death) blows its chill wind under the door. So, as he had always done, Gautier longed for a warm, exotic climate.

In *Emaux et camées* the poet's Eden is carefully constructed around the Mediterranean area. The blue of water and sky suggests the ideal (blue being nearly always a symbol of the ideal in nineteenth-century literature), and at the same time the water itself permits Gautier to concretize his ideal in the figure of Venus rising from the waves.

> Le sein de perles ruisselant,
> La Vénus de l'Adriatique [i.e., Venice]
> Sort de l'eau son corps rose et bleu. (p. 16)

(Her bosom dripping pearls,/The Venus of the Adriatic [i.e., Venice]/Comes out of the water, her body pink and blue.)

And in "Le Poème de la femme" he compares a beautiful woman to a Venus posing naked at the edge of the sea.

With the centrality of the feminine image established, Gautier selected three of his favorite geographical areas (besides Venice) to express different aspects of man's encounter with the feminine ideal: Spain, the Near East, and Greece. Sometimes the entire poem is set in one of these exotic locales, but frequently Gautier preferred to insert just one quatrain evoking one of his idealized paradises into a modern setting in an attempt to reinforce the beauty of the woman who had inspired the poem. But whether fragment or entire poem, Gautier's vision of these Mediterranean lands remains consistent.

In his Spanish poems fiery passion is the dominant motif and red the appropriate color, as a strophe from "Carmen" indicates:

> Et parmi sa pâleur éclate
> Une bouche aux rires vainqueurs;
> Piment rouge, fleur écarlate,
> Qui prend sa pourpre au sang des coeurs.

(And in the midst of her pallor there explodes/A mouth with its conquering laughter;/A red pepper, a scarlet flame,/That takes its crimson color from the heart's blood.)

When Gautier moves to the other end of the Mediterranean, he revels in the mystery and sensuality of the East. In "Ce que disent les hirondelles" ("What the Swallows Say") the birds going south for the winter are a metaphor for the poet's longing ("car le poète est un oiseau"). One dreams of Smyrna where "the Hadjis count their grains of amber/On the threshold warmed by a ray of sunshine." In "La Fellah" an Egyptian peasant girl, half hidden by her veil, seems infinitely attractive:

> L'antique Isis légua ses voiles
> Aux modernes filles du Nil;
> Mais, sous le bandeau, deux étoiles
> Brillent d'un feu pur et subtil.

(Ancient Isis bequeathed her veils/To the modern girls of the Nile;/But beneath the strip of cloth, two stars/Shine with pure and subtle fire.)

In "Le Poème de la femme" Gautier describes

> La Georgienne indolente
> Avec son souple narguilhé,
> Etalant sa hanche opulente,
> Un pied sous l'autre replié.

(The indolent Georgian woman/With her supple water pipe,/Displaying her opulent hip,/One foot bent under the other.)

Each of these Oriental scenes is characterized by a total immobility or stasis which makes a sharp contrast with the feverish agitation of life in a Western capital.

Gautier's third idealized country, ancient Greece, inevitably permits the poet to conjure up the marvels of Classical art:

> Dans le fronton d'un temple antique,
> Deux blocs de marbre ont, trois mille ans,
> Sur le fond bleu du ciel attique
> Juxtaposé leurs rêves blancs.

(In the pediment of an ancient temple,/Two blocks of marble have for three thousand years,/Against the blue backdrop of the Attic sky/Juxtaposed their white dreams.)

But of course Greece sooner or later suggests to Gautier the sculptured female form. In "Le Poème de la femme" a woman is "un marbre de chair" ("flesh which seems to be marble"), and in his Parisian "Fantaisies d'hiver" ("Winter Fantasy") he reminds his reader of the Greek ideal by describing the statues of Venus and Phocion in the Tuileries gardens.

There is one important poem, often anthologized, in *Emaux et camées* which is not Mediterranean in its setting but which serves as a fitting conclusion to this section, for in it we find concentrated the themes and images that express Gautier's longing for a world of pure form, and yet we also find the poet's awareness of its limitations. "Symphonie en blanc majeur" ("Symphony in White Major") is an interesting attempt to play with the nuances of the color white. The central figure (inspired by Marie Kalergis, wife of the Danish ambassador) is a woman dressed in white, whose skin seems whiter still. Each strophe asks whether she was formed of one white substance or another. The poet begins with white snow maidens of Nordic legend, and then he describes arctic glaciers. Moving south, he finds comparisons first with camelias, then with marble and ivory. The constantly reiterated idea is that the woman is perfect but inhuman, and Gautier's eternal debate between the ideal and the real surfaces in the final stanza:

Sous la glace où calme il repose,
Oh! qui pourra fondre ce coeur!
Oh! qui pourra mettre un ton rose
Dans cette implacable blancheur!

(Under the ice where it rests quietly,/Oh, who could melt that heart!/Oh, who could put a pink tint/Into that implacable whiteness!)

As John Van Eerde put it, "Gautier apparently becomes shocked at the cold uniform white of his own creation."[6] As we have seen time after time, whenever Gautier had too much of the daily grind, he longed for the ideal, but after excessive contemplation of the ideal in the world of his own imagination, he often felt the need to return to the real and the human.

Taken as a whole, these poems in *Emaux et camées* show that whatever ideal paradise Gautier selected, whatever real woman may have served as the inspiration for his poem, he quickly transformed both place and person so that they represent ways of overcoming the impermanence of Western culture. In Spain, as the title "Carmen" suggests, passionate love leads to death, and the same idea is present in another major Spanish poem, "Inez de las Sierras," based on a story by Charles Nodier. But passion and death in these poems are not entirely negative. They represent absolutes of experience that serve to suggest how paltry is the cautious bourgeois practicality of the modern Western world. The immobile mystery of the East, the sculptured purity of Greek art, and the white of Northern snows have a different tone but serve the same purpose. Their very immobility and purity point to something more desirable and more permanent than the West can give.

But even though *Emaux et camées* has meaning and is not an "empty" volume as some critics have claimed, a majority of the poems fail to give the reader the feeling that he is reading great poetry. What makes great poetry is impossible to demonstrate, for there is magic in art. But one can feel it. All one has to do is to turn to other poets of the century, not only to giants like Hugo and Baudelaire, but even, to mention only three of widely varying technique and vision, to Verlaine, Rimbaud, and Hérédia, and one can sense the difference. Because the magic is often lacking in Gautier's *Emaux et camées* (despite Jasinski's admiration), it is not hard to understand the widespread lack of enthusiasm of contemporary critics for this poetry. To be less impressionistic and more analytical, we can conclude by suggesting one logical reason for the weakness of this poetry. The themes of escape to a more pleasing world need a form which has enough scope to encompass this expansiveness. In his Egyptian stories Gautier showed that he was capable of opening up his vision into that "expansion des choses infinies" that Baudelaire recommended in "Correspondances." But in *Emaux et camées* Gautier consciously reined in his imagination. Perhaps it was a fear of becoming pompously overblown ("Le Roman de la momie" shows that the danger was real), or perhaps it was a fear of giving himself up totally to his own dreams, as Gérard de Nerval had done. In any case, there seems little doubt that on the whole the restrictive form and the vast longing for the ideal are out of phase with each other.

III *Later Poetry*

After 1852 Gautier continued to write poetry that was not destined for inclusion in the revised editions of *Emaux et camées*. A large majority of these efforts were published at one time or another, however. A few, commissioned by the government of Napoleon III for state occasions, appeared in *Le Moniteur universel*. Some sonnets inspired by Marie Mattéi appeared in the second series of *Le Parnasse contemporain* in 1870. A large group of poems written for his friend and patroness, Princess Mathilde, was published in a very limited edition and presented to her as a birthday gift in 1869. Emile Bergerat published others, including some poems to Carlotta Grisi, after the poet's death. Many of these poems were included in a posthumous edition of Gautier's *Poésies complètes* (1875 - 76). Others, especially incomplete fragments of poems, were available for a long time only in Spoelberch de Lovenjoul's *Histoire des oeuvres de Théophile Gautier*. Thanks to René Jasinski's recent edition of Gautier's complete poetry, these later works are now more readily accessible. They appear in a final group of more than sixty poems with the title "Dernières poésies."[7]

If today's reader finds little to appreciate in this collection, the reason is no doubt due to changing tastes. In the French Classical period, especially in the eighteenth century, a great deal of poetry was occasional, that is, written for a lady's birthday or at the request of some court figure who paid the poet to flatter him. In this kind of verse the conceit played a large role. A charming epigram or clever compliment was frequently the point of the exercise. It is widely supposed that this kind of cerebral approach to poetry was swept away by the Romantic revolution, which demanded a display of genuine sentiment expressed through the power of the creative imagination. But in fact the older tradition was maintained even into the early twentieth century, with guest books providing the opportunity to pen a witty quatrain to one's host. In nineteenth-century France the keepsake, similar in nature, was a standard institution.

Gautier's later verse is primarily occasional, and on the whole modern readers consider the poetry shallow and little more than an excuse for demonstrating the poet's cleverness. One of the sonnets to Marie Mattéi is typical. Entitled "La Fumée" ("Smoke"), it tells of the poet's ride with her in the Bois de Boulogne. In the final tercet he lights up a cigar and she a *papelito,* and the final line explains the title: "Et l'Amour, pour voile, a cette fumée" (And Love has this smoke for a veil). To end a love sonnet by transforming tobacco smoke into a protective shield for the lovers may be novel, charming, and slightly amusing, but the vision rather lacks depth, even if it did serve its purpose, which was to entertain and delight Marie.

Another form of verse that Gautier indulged in was a kind of after-dinner game. It consisted of *bouts-rimés,* which were poems that one was to write within a given time period in a preconceived rhyme scheme. There are seventeen of these included in Jasinski's edition. An extreme example of this type is a sonnet written by Gautier for his daughter Estelle (in 1871 or 1872). A real tour de force, it not only accepts the challenge of the rhymes at the end of each line, but the first letter of each line, read vertically, forms the name ESTELLE GAUTIER. This clever facility recalls the *grands rhétoriqueurs* of the fifteenth century, who also indulged in acrostics and other artificially difficult exercises. One can appreciate the wit and the talent, but modern taste usually leads us in other directions.

Curiously, among all this rather mediocre verse, there is one very remarkable sonnet entitled "L'Impassible." To understand its place in the development of Gautier's poetry, however, we must first return to *Emaux et camées* to examine a poem, "Coerulei Oculi" (which can mean both "Dark Blue Eyes" and "Sea-Green Eyes"), which in a very real sense anticipates it, in that it shows a technique quite different from Gautier's usual one. Normally in his poetry Gautier presents a world of reality or a world of fantasy, and the reader has no trouble knowing exactly where he is. If in some poems we find both worlds (just as in the fantastic tales), the texts are usually divided into clearly separable parts, and the reader knows when he moves from one to the other. But "Coerulei Oculi" (1852) shows no such obvious dualism and is more delicately ambiguous.

For this poem Gautier moved away from the clear light and blue water of the Mediterranean to the murkier green seas of northern Europe. He creates a heroine in harmony with the setting:

Une femme mystérieuse,
Dont la beauté trouble mes sens,
Se tient debout, silencieuse,
Au bord des flots retentissants.

Ses yeux, où le ciel se reflète,
Mêlent à leur azur amer,
Qu'étoile une humide paillette,
Les teintes glauques de la mer.

(A mysterious woman/Whose beauty disturbs my senses,/Stands silently/At the edge of the resounding sea./Her eyes, in which the sky is reflected,/Mingle in with their bitter blue/Starred with flecks of moist gold/The sea-green tints of the sea.)

The scene is constructed with delicately balanced ambiguity. Blue represents frank openness, but the woman's eyes are also sea-green, which suggests attractive but dangerous mysteries as unfathomable as the ocean itself. The two worlds of sea and sky blend totally for one moment as the poet refers to the mingling of the "bitter blue" of her eyes with the green tints of the sea. This phrase not only suggests the blending of the salty sea with the pure blue of the sky, but on another level, the idea that any encounter with this mysterious woman will be a bittersweet experience. Even the subtle, shifting rhythms with which the poem opens contribute to the overall tone. In the French the first line starts slowly, then accelerates (the line is divided into two groups of three and five syllables, and the larger group is read at a faster rate). The second line repeats the acceleration in the first half, but then the second half breaks into two groups (one and three syllables) and ends more slowly with a drop in pitch. The rhythm is like a wave cresting, cresting again, and then breaking up. The last two lines are evenly balanced, but the rising and falling inflections suggest, again like waves about to break, that the equilibrium can only be a momentary one.

The subtlety and the ambiguities do not end here. In the narrative of the poem the man looks into the woman's eyes, and his soul is drawn into their depths. Then the poet compares her to the siren who had enticed King Harald Harfagar of ancient Norway, and soon the woman has become a siren who lures the narrator into the sea where he drowns (or his heart does; it is hard to be sure) as he consummates his union with her. So we are left wondering which is the reality, the woman on the shore or the siren in the sea. By the poem's end it is not easy to tell. Is the experience creative or destructive? The surrender to the woman's power ends in literal or metaphoric death, but the poem contains references to the treasures that can be found in the depths of the sea. This haunting poem closes with as much or even more mystery than at its beginning. In *La Comédie de la mort* Gautier had already been preoccupied with themes that Baudelaire would later find congenial. But here Gautier is experimenting with Baudelaire's technique of blending reality and dream, of confusing object and metaphor.

In "L'Impassible" Gautier took the technique of creating ambiguity by blending different elements into one and carried it a step further. As the poem is brief, we quote it in its entirety.

> La Satiété dort au fond de vos grands yeux;
> En eux plus de désirs, plus d'amour, plus d'envie;
> Ils ont bu la lumière, ils ont tari la vie,
> Comme une mer profonde où s'absorbent les cieux.
>
> Sous leur bleu sombre on lit le vaste ennui des Dieux,
> Pour qui toute chimère est d'avance assouvie,
> Et qui, sachant l'effet dont la cause est suivie,
> Mélangent au présent l'avenir déjà vieux.
>
> L'infini s'est fondu dans vos larges prunelles,
> Et devant ce miroir qui ne réfléchit rien,
> L'Amour découragé s'asseoit, fermant ses ailes.
>
> Vous, cependant, avec un calme olympien,
> Comme la Mnémosyne à son socle accoudée,
> Vous poursuivez, rêveuse, une impossible idée.[8]

In this sonnet Gautier repeats the major motifs of "Coerulei oculi." In both we find the alluring woman in whose eyes the poet sees the infinite sea. While the masochistic desire to be annihilated voluptuously by a superior and indifferent woman is more pronounced in "Coerulei oculi," both poems are based on the idea of the woman's superiority and the man's passivity. The Baudelairean qualities of this sonnet are derived not only from its decadent themes, which cannot fail to remind one of "Sed non satiata" or "La Beauté," but also from the fact that Gautier again puts ambiguity at the heart of the poem. We never learn the nature of the "impossible idea" that haunts the central figure, with the result that each reader stops to wonder what it might be and can thus "complete" the vision with the richness of his own dreams.

Even more advanced in this poem is Gautier's technique of handling time. In the first stanza we learn that all possibilities for action have been exhausted, that all human effort is over for the woman (line 3), and that past acts have been absorbed through memory into an eternal present. In like manner the second stanza reveals that any wish for the future is satisfied in advance. Thus both past and future blend into one vast totality (line 8). In abolishing the three distinct time periods the woman has in a sense overcome the limitations that make us finite and mortal and become infinite herself. Her awareness of totality makes her a kind of goddess, able, as we see at the poem's end, to dream on a scale beyond that of ordinary people. This poem has attracted widespread acclaim and has even been compared favorably to some of Baudelaire's finest creations (like "Le Flacon" and "La Chevelure"), for the author of *Les Fleurs du mal* often used the technique of unifying past, present, and future time, combining it with a central ambiguity to achieve the same effect of liberating the reader's vision. Gautier's discovery of the possibilities of the unity of time, incidentally, was a more positive way of overcoming the fragmentation of modern life than to escape to imaginary worlds where the problem did not exist.

Curiously, the lady for whom "L'Impassible" was written was left quite indifferent by Gautier's tribute. She must have sensed that the poem was no mere bouquet to her charms and that the process of artistic transformation had left her far behind, but her indifference is the modern reader's delight.

To assess Gautier as a poet is a difficult task. If to Baudelaire he is the "impeccable poet" of the dedication of *Les Fleurs du mal*, most critics today are much less complimentary, and American college courses in French literature rarely offer his poetry to undergraduates. Gautier shared Baudelaire's pessimism concerning life and his hostility to progress as well as his dedication to beauty and to art. But ideas alone do not make a poet great. Except on the rare occasions discussed above, Gautier did not develop the techniques that would have permitted him to interpenetrate the real and the ideal, blending past and present time in a subtle fusion. Gautier was a good poet and on a few occasions rose to the greatest heights, but normally the magic of the very greatest poetry is lacking. In fact, despite all his feeling that prose was drudgery and that poetry was his true calling, Gautier was actually a better prose writer than a poet. "Spirite" has finer lyricism than most of his verse, and in our final chapter we shall examine his prose masterpiece, *Le Capitaine Fracasse*.

CHAPTER 8

Le Capitaine Fracasse

I *Genesis*

THÉOPHILE Gautier had been planning to write *Le Capitaine Fracasse* (1863) (best translated perhaps as *Captain Braggart)* ever since 1835, and its forthcoming publication was announced as early as 1836. We do not know today exactly what Gautier intended his story to be during the 1830's, and it is possible that he did not have a clear idea either. All we know for certain is that in those years of his youth he again and again spoke of his weariness with the "monotonous" literature of the late seventeenth century and his delight in the earlier era of Louis XIII. The first half of "le grand siècle"appealed to him and to his fellow Romantics because of its verve, its sense of freedom, and its opportunities for heroic action. When Gautier spoke fondly of a "Louis XIII style," he meant a style appropriate to the age, one that was rich and exuberant, "full of grand Castillian expressions, of those fine ways of a gentleman which give it a large and magnificent form. The sentence falls in ample folds, like those ancient rich cloths embroidered with gold and silver, but without any stiffness."[1] The following passage, taken from an article on the poet Théophile de Viau, will serve to illustrate what he meant, even if the style in fact owes more to Chateaubriand than to the seventeenth century:

> It was a Louis XIII park in all its splendor. . . . There were brick terraces with stone corners, large open flowers in marble vases, gently sloping balustrades with fat balusters. . . . One could see through the trees and behind the arbors tame deer, white as snow, running about; partridges and pheasants, as if at home, wandered along the walls with their entire brood . . . [and] out on the pond a few swans paddled indolently, their necks curved, their wings open. It was a paradise that would make one disgusted with the original one. It was one of those beautiful dreams evoked by poets and painters in the evening when they see the sun setting behind the tall chestnut trees.[2]

But as we saw in an earlier chapter, *Mademoiselle de Maupin* had already offered Gautier the possibility of writing an historical romance full of daring and bravado, yet Gautier had preferred to speculate on beauty, love and permanence. He was apparently not ready to write a popular adventure tale in the tradition of Vigny's *Cinq-Mars*. A decade later, in March 1846, the *Revue des deux mondes* announced the imminent publication of the work and even gave Gautier an advance on royalties. But the procrastinating poet never wrote a line, and the director of the journal, François Buloz, understandably angry, asked for his money back. When Gautier failed to reimburse him, Buloz sued. The affair dragged on for a while, and in 1853 just as Gautier's wages were to be attached, help appeared from an unexpected quarter. The financier Jules Mirès, long an admirer of Gautier's work, paid the poet's debt, and the suit, now moot, was dropped.

With Buloz pacified, Gautier decided to offer *Le Capitaine Fracasse* to the *Revue de Paris*, and once again there was an announcement of its forthcoming publication. But once again nothing came of it. Boschot believes that Gautier got no further than the first chapter, which he probably wrote in 1857 or 1858.[3] Finally, on Christmas day of 1861, the *Revue nationale* published the first chapter. Had the entire story been written by then, publication of the more than twenty chapters would have taken ten or eleven months, as the journal appeared bimonthly. But in fact publication took a year and a half, which more than suggests that Gautier was writing it as it was published. This surmise is supported by Gautier's daughter, Judith, who later wrote that the editor, Georges Charpentier, knowing Gautier's casual ways, refused him any advances and paid him twenty francs for each sheet as it came in, stamping each one with the word "paid" in purple ink.[4] The story was finally finished and appeared in book form in 1863. The long delay between the initial idea and the published volume was not without value, however. Gautier at the age of fifty was physically sluggish and no longer possessed the energy of youth. But what he had lost in vigor, he had more than gained in maturity and command of the writer's craft. What had been originally conceived as a simple adventure tale turned out to be his masterpiece.

II *The Romance*

There are some literary sources for *Le Capitaine Fracasse*. Gautier obviously owes a few details to Scarron's seventeenth-century *Le*

Roman comique, and a scene or two perhaps to an early tale by Gérard de Nerval entitled "Le Prince des sots" ("The Prince of Fools"). But these are not very important. What provides the basic structure of Gautier's story is the long tradition of the romance. This literary genre, whose tradition in France goes back to the Middle Ages, had fallen into disrepute among eighteenth-century intellectuals. When Voltaire, for instance, referred to a *roman*, he meant what modern criticism calls a romance. He was thinking of the popular adventure story of his day, and the lack of verisimilitude of these tales so annoyed him that he refused to call his own stories *romans*. He even took his revenge upon the genre by parodying it savagely in *Candide*. But with the Romantics there was a brief revival of the genre. In England Ann Radcliffe's "Gothic novels" were in fact romances, as was essentially the fiction of Sir Walter Scott. Both writers became popular on the continent in the 1820's. But the romance was soon submerged by the realistic novel with its sociological and psychological realism, with the result that the romance as a genre became so discredited — because of its alleged "falsity" — that a work like *Le Capitaine Fracasse* is popular today only among adolescents in France who like to read adventure stories. Yet the genre stubbornly survives. Movies (such as the classic American Western), comic strip adventures, and detective stories in print or on television have in today's world become the province of this "forgotten" genre.

To what may we attribute the survival of romance, still a favorite with the average person even if scorned by sociologists and intellectuals? It hardly suffices to claim arrogantly that the stupidity of the text is in perfect harmony with that of the reader-viewer. In fact, as Jungian psychology suggests, romances seem to be a projection of the masculine part of each person's psyche (whether called animus, libido, or something else) on to the hero, the feminine part on to the heroine, and the evil or "shadow" in us on to the villain. The drama acted out in literature (comedy and melodrama in the theater; the romance in prose) wherein the villain is overcome and the hero and heroine are married is a metaphor for the elimination within ourselves of the psychological blocking agent that interferes with the harmonious fusion of the two elements of our personality. In a normal romance the happy ending is the necessary outcome, and the final marriage represents the creation of an integrated being, while the promise of children to be born to the happy couple predicts our own future creativity now that we are in harmony with ourselves.

Our satisfaction with the ending of the typical romance reflects our need for an inner peace that will permit us to be personally and socially creative.

But romances have one major problem. With the plots so unvarying in their essentials, there tends to be a terrible sameness to them all. To vary the formula the romancer needs to introduce some fresh element to disguise his fundamental plot. One common technique is to vary the locale, to find a place or a period in past time that seems "real" but is remote enough so that it may be at least partly transformed into an idealized society or landscape. As Northrop Frye puts it, "the popular demand in fiction is . . . for a . . . novel just romantic enough for the reader to project his libido on the hero and his anima on the heroine, and just novel enough to keep these projections in a familiar world."[5] Should the world become totally unfamiliar, we have passed into the realm of myth, as with Tolkien, or into science fiction.

Another method for varying the basic pattern is through the insertion of ideology. The ideas presented in romances are nearly always simple and are attached to the principal characters. *Ivanhoe*, for instance, associates the hero with Saxon virtue and the villain with Norman evil. In the mid-twentieth century, unrealistic Soviet romances (under the misleading label of Stalinist realism) provide a more modern example of simplistic characters created to serve a political ideology. Given what we know of Théophile Gautier's desire for political noninvolvement, we are not surprised to discover that he refrained from taking any controversial political stance in *Le Capitaine Fracasse*. There is perhaps a moment's doubt concerning the monarchy when the hero is disenchanted upon seeing the king for the first time. But Gautier is careful not to overdo his criticism, for traditionally, historical romances require a hierarchical, even a feudal structure for the hero's exploits. In trying to vary the basic formula, Gautier chose to describe the period of Louis XIII with all its local color, but this detail, while interesting, adds nothing to what a Scott or a Vigny had already done, and Gautier was eager to write something more significant.

For years he had been articulating his dissatisfaction with the real, and in the majority of his narratives he had by one means or another managed to place his hero in some kind of paradise. But ever since he had written "Celle-ci et celle-là," Gautier had been intellectually aware that the quest for the ideal was certain to lead to frustration and disappointment. His trip to Spain in 1840 brought this truth home to him on an emotional level, but so great was his desire for the absolute that he nonetheless continued to write stories that dealt with idealized characters in idealized settings. If Gautier intended "Spirite" to be a kind of final tribute to the ideal, he planned *Le Capitaine Fracasse* as his final statement about the multiple illusions and realities of existence. His romance is in essence a transformation of the voyage to Spain into a purely fictive form, as if to show through a more generalized hero that not just he, Théophile Gautier, began life full of bright illusions which were ultimately destroyed by time, but that we all experience this fate. The romance form with its promise of a happy ending was curiously suited to Gautier's pessimistic message. Everything about a romance points to the hero's final victory. To follow the formula of the typical romance until near the end and suddenly reveal that the whole quest for happiness is doomed to failure creates an irony of considerable impact. Although Gautier clearly planned to deceive his average reader until just before the end, he intended also to plant a few clues along the way that might alert a "happy few" to what was to be the final outcome.

As if mindful of Frye's injunction to include enough "reality" to make his fictional world familiar, Gautier is careful at the outset to situate his tale in time (the early seventeenth century) and place (between Dax and Mont-de-Marsan in southwestern France), and as the story progresses, we find other bits of local color — roadside inns with beaten earthen floors typical of the period, the poor state of the roads, thieves' dens in Paris, and so forth. Similarly, there is some element of realism when Gautier presents his hero, Baron Sigognac. The young man lives in an old dilapidated castle with the sole company of a cat, a dog, a horse, and an old manservant. Gautier explains that at that time it was far from rare to find noble families impoverished by carelessness or profligacy. A common solution of that day was to go to Paris and appeal to the king for an opportunity to rebuild the family estate, but Gautier has us understand that there was the danger of the nobleman's degenerating into a mere courtier, and so from pride as well as timidity, Sigognac has refused.

Social realism, whether of the roads or of the hero's fortunes, however, remains superficial and secondary. What we really have is the typical romance pattern of the impoverished hero out to make his fortune. To reinforce this idea Gautier surrounds Sigognac with dismal trappings of barrenness. As the story opens, it is almost winter. The castle is infested with toads and spiders. Nettles, hemlock, and poisonous mushrooms grow everywhere, and in open symbolism a statue of Pomona, the goddess of fruit trees, is covered with scale and has a missing nose, like death itself. Indoors, worms crawl in and out of the woodwork. The whole place is like the abandoned castle of Sleeping Beauty where "the cadaver of the past crumbled slowly into dust in these rooms where the present never set foot" (p. 9).

We recall that in myth and romance there is inevitably a "call to adventure"[6] that starts the story on its way. Here it is provided by the unexpected arrival of a wandering troupe of actors seeking shelter for the night. Their repertoire is limited and traditional, with the usual stock characters. There is, of course, a young lover and his beloved. There is also a coquette, a witty maid, an old lady, a king, a pedant, and a *miles gloriosus,* or braggart soldier. Sigognac is charmed by the group, especially by the beautiful ingenue Isabelle, and realizing that his life is without meaning if he stays alone within his walls, he accepts an invitation to join the troupe as it heads toward Paris, where he may be able to recoup his fortunes. This positive decision, as is fitting in a world of romance, is accompanied by sudden presages of good fortune. The weather promptly cooperates. The storm of the night before turns into a refreshing rain (p. 48), and rain is the water image most typically associated with springtime, the season of renewal. Gautier describes the scene: "The reeds, green again, swung their golden flowers; the water plants spread themselves out over the surface of the refreshed ponds; even the pines shook their dark foliage less funereally and gave forth an odor of resin; little blue puffs of smoke rose gaily from a copse of chestnut trees" (p. 48). But even with this encouragement the baron hesitates to accept the call to a new life, for all men fear the unknown, and like them Sigognac is attached to the familiar past, in his case the old castle. But Isabelle's influence is so strong that he decides to cross the threshold, and with that act "the sorrow on Sigognac's face vanished like a cloud broken apart by a ray of sunshine" (p. 51).

Because Gautier uses every known technique of the romance tradition, we can almost guess what will happen next. We are certain that a villain will appear to threaten the heroine, and we can guess equally well that the hero will prove to be a fine swordsman and defeat him. We might also predict that the heroine, who is presented as the illegitimate daughter of an actress now dead and an unknown great nobleman, will find her father, be legitimized, and marry the hero and live happily ever after. This is, after all, what romances are all about. There is an aura of predictability, even of inevitability to the genre, and we are not surprised to read on occasion the suggestion that fate is playing a hand in the story.

But as we suggested above, under the comfortable, predictable façade of the romance, there is great uncertainty about life and about reality and our illusions. This idea first becomes apparent when the actors arrive at Sigognac's castle. The device of introducing a troupe of actors (derived from Scarron's *Le Roman comique)* is ideal for playing on illusion and reality, for actors by their very profession are creators of real illusions, and as for their characters, the roles they play on stage may or may not reflect their true natures. Isabelle is as pure as she seems, and the pedant talks pedantically on stage and off, but the young lover of the troupe, Léandre, is in fact neither a perfect lover nor a true hero but a well-dressed fop eager for conquests among the noble ladies who come to watch the plays. The braggart soldier, so cowardly on stage, is in real life a decent enough fellow. That all this is a parable of the real world is made clear: "The actor's van contains an entire world, and in truth, isn't theater life on a small scale" (p. 92)? So Gautier has asked his first question — are we what we appear as we strut on the stage of life? — and he makes no clear answer. Some are, some are not.

But the probing goes deeper. On the whole, nineteenth-century social novelists like Balzac tended to assume that reality was a solid constant and that man's problem was less to know what it was than to take a stance in relation to it. But we know from Gautier's fantastic tales and his general belief in superstitions that he was at times haunted by the unknown that might lie behind the façade or illusion of reality. A suggestion of this idea occurs early in *Le Capitaine Fracasse* when "frightening" pictures of family ancestors in the old castle take on "because of the decomposition of the colors, the appearance of ghouls" (p. 6). A few pages later a tapestry takes on livid hues in the flickering lamplight, and a figure woven into the cloth becomes "almost real." One would have thought it a "vampire dripping with blood." These details are more than borrowings from the Gothic novel to heighten suspense; they are preparations for his ending that our life is not to be predicted in any comfortable way. The experiences are not always gruesome, however. Baron Sigognac's early intimations of the uncertain quality of life when the actors first come to his castle are very pleasant. Suddenly in the presence of pretty women, he has the feeling "of being in a dream . . . constantly afraid that he would wake up" (p. 25). Here, what seems illusion — his "dream" — is in fact reality within the fiction.

A more complex experience awaits the hero soon after leaving the castle. The troupe is ambushed by a highwayman, Agostino, and what appears to be his band of a half dozen brigands. Sigognac, alert for trouble, sees them, but because the figures are immobile, assumes they are not men but tree stumps, and relaxes. When Agostino emerges from hiding and halts the troupe, Sigognac realizes that his initial judgment was faulty and belatedly springs into action to save the troupe, only to discover the real reality of the encounter. The assisting brigands who appear to be stumps are in a sense stumps. They are stuffed dummies that Agostino must use to intimidate his prospective victims, because the original brigands have long since died or been put in prison. The encounter turns comic as Agostino is quickly disarmed, but the humorous nature of this episode in no way undercuts the lesson — sometimes what we think is true is an illusion, but then the illusion turns out to have a deeper level of truth after all. The comic is soon abandoned for the serious, however, as shortly afterwards winter weather sets in and the troupe is caught in a raging blizzard. The function of the snowstorm is not to suggest any death of love, for Sigognac and Isabelle are happy with each other despite the snow. It is rather to associate death with the decomposition of reality. Gautier's remarkable description of the snow is reminiscent of Melville's chapter in *Moby Dick* on the White Horror. Under the harsh, whirling wind and the driving snow, reality comes apart: "The snowflakes rose, fell, crisscrossed, yet without touching the ground or landing anywhere . . . becoming so thick that they formed a white darkness. . . . In this silvery swarm of flakes even the nearest objects lost their real outline and were no longer recognizable" (p. 142). The actors, now on foot to spare their one tired horse, disappear into the white chaos, and when one of them, the braggart soldier, is not seen again, the others go to find him. Penetrating the unknown, they finally find him dead, frozen stiff. They bury him a little later in an obscure plot of earth, obliged to drive away mangy curs and having themselves to flee an attack by hostile villagers. There seems to be a lesson in this episode, one that confirms Gautier's lifelong pessimism. When the surface reality of life is blotted out, when our comfortable world decomposes, we disappear into an unknown, and then when the swirl of confusion is cleared away, our body lies there grotesque in death, abandoned by a hostile society.

The theme of illusion and reality, already announced by the very presence of a troupe of actors, is further explored when Sigognac himself becomes an actor to replace the dead man, who had played the role of the braggart soldier. As the hero is anything but cowardly, he must, paradoxically, be false to his own nature to communicate the truth of his role. Sigognac develops a technique that combines the artificial and the natural. Although calm inside, he must project the wildest fury when playing in a farce like *Les Rhodomontades du Capitaine Fracasse* ("The Vain Blustering of Captain Braggart"). Yet Sigognac wants the audience "to discern the man under the puppet" (p. 204). So he varies his voice to include both natural and unnatural tones, and he wears only a half-mask, which represents both the illusion of his role and the reality of his person. The result of this artful combination of the natural and the artificial is that spectators take the action on the stage as true (p. 179). Some illusion, then, is necessary to communicate a sense of the real. Later one of the actors takes the idea a step further when he says, "After all, since the stage is the mirror of life, life should resemble it the way a man resembles his portrait" (p. 428). Which, then, Gautier seems to be asking, is the greater illusion or the greater reality, art or life?

These speculations on the ambiguities of reality are somewhat muted when the villain finally appears and the normal patterns of romance take over. The villain is divinely beautiful in a Byronic way, but since the author immediately takes the reader into his confidence, we know that the man is pure evil. Even his name, the Duke of Vallombreuse (or Shadowy Valley) makes clear that he is a symbol of death. He collects women as objects, becoming their lover, then cajoling them into having a nude miniature painted of them, and finally, bored, he throws them out. He takes on the stock attributes of the villain, grinding his teeth with rage when foiled and hiring vulgar criminals to do his dirty work. There is perhaps a suggestion of something deeper beneath the banal characterization. He has that sense of the absolute so frequent in Gautier. He laments that all his conquests are too facile because of his supreme beauty. It is as if his very perfection has corrupted him and made him evil. He stands as a warning against achieving one's absolute dream because of the very inhuman and unfeeling person one may then become.

When the troupe reaches Paris the motif of the decomposition of reality reappears. The people swarming in the streets (p. 293) are distantly analogous to snowflakes swirling in a blizzard. One must penetrate the confusion to understand the realities beneath. Fortunately, the hero has a guide, the pedant, who knows Paris well and shows him how to avoid the lurking cutpurses and paid killers. Thus when Vallombreuse reappears (the hero had wounded him in a duel in the provinces and put him out of action for a few weeks), the hero is ready and manages to avoid or neutralize the attacks made on him. But one cannot always unmask illusion for what it is, as the next episode makes clear. It was common for actors to be invited to the country houses of the nobility, and the troupe is unsuspecting when invited away from Paris to perform. On the way to a nonexistent domain they are ambushed by Vallombreuse. The heroine is taken off to the villain's lair where he intends, to use the language of melodrama, to bend her to his will.

In the nick of time a young bandit girl, Chiquita, whom the hero had earlier befriended, is able to inform Sigognac of his beloved's location. He arrives with his friends, assaults the castle, and saves the heroine after killing Vallombreuse in a final battle. It looks as if all will end happily, for at this moment Vallombreuse's distinguished father appears (it is his castle), and we learn, thanks to the usual ring that permits a typical recognition scene, that Isabelle is his long lost daughter, and he restores her to her rightful rank and fortune. Isabelle had thought herself a commoner and was reluctant to marry Sigognac because she felt socially unworthy of him, but now all barriers appear to be removed, and the reader is prepared for the happy ending.

III *The Two Endings*

It is at this point that Gautier springs his surprise. His idea was to show that the very acts of living, even those that create our happiness, are precisely those which cause our ultimate downfall. Balzac had already toyed with something similar in *La Peau de chagrin* ("The Wild Ass's Skin"), whose lesson was that to really live we need to exercise the will, but that very exercise of our will eventually burns us out and causes our death. In his turn Gautier had planned a bitter ending to *Le Capitaine Fracasse* that would reveal the inescapable irony of life. We see it on the secondary level in the case of Agostino. His joy in life had been highway robbery, and what made his life happy caused its end. He is captured and broken on the wheel. But Gautier reserved the main thrust of his irony for the hero. We know that Sigognac will never truly come alive if he refuses the quest in the first place, but once embarked upon it, he must destroy the villain both to win the girl and to stay alive, but since the villain is the heroine's brother, a marriage between her and his killer is unthinkable in the eyes of them all. Trapped by his own unavoidable successes, Sigognac — as Gautier planned the story — sees his dream fade to nothing. Utterly defeated, he limps back to his castle and there drags out a short, miserable life until death claims him and his animals. To lose is bad enough, but to lose because of one's very successes underscores the hopelessness of all human effort.

An unhappy conclusion is upsetting enough to the general public, but when it is grafted on to the patterns of romance that cry out for a happy ending, a tragic ending becomes almost intolerable. When Gautier's friends and family learned what the ending was to be, they were stunned. They had missed the ironies and subtle clues along the way and begged him to change the ending. So did his publisher, Georges Charpentier, who feared that the book would not sell. Gautier finally yielded to their entreaties and rewrote the ending.[7]

He must have rewritten it quickly, for the second ending is not smoothly welded to the text. Even after Gautier completed his rewriting, Vallombreuse is referred to, not as near death or hovering between life and death, but as actually dead for several pages. "There is a corpse between us," moans Sigognac. "I myself created the obstacle that would destroy my love and I killed my hope with my sword which was defending my beloved. In order to keep the one I loved, I lost her forever" (p. 418). On the following pages Vallombreuse is several times referred to as dead. But finally the second ending takes over, we learn that a doctor is on the way and that perhaps all is not lost. After some suspenseful moments, Vallombreuse recovers. Meanwhile, as planned in the first version, a disconsolate Sigognac has headed home thinking he has lost Isabelle forever.

To solve the problem of the villain's death was not Gautier's only problem. He also had to decide what to do with him now that he was saved. He had been constantly presented as a naturally cruel man. But a happy ending needs a harmonious society. So either Vallombreuse must go off to the wars or to America or he must change. Against all verisimilitude he changes and becomes the most considerate of brothers and the most likeable of brothers-in-law. Noticing that Isabelle is pining away without Sigognac, he travels to the southwest and brings the hero back in order to make possible the inevitable wedding.

If the story had ended at this point, we would have had the

traditional ending of a romance. But Gautier added some extra flourishes at the end. After a few months the newlyweds go south to Sigognac's castle and upon their arrival find it and its gardens completely restored to their original splendor. The explanation given is that Isabelle, now wealthy, has had the castle secretly repaired, but the time span allotted is far too short for any such restoration to have really taken place. Indeed, as Gautier presents it, there is something almost magical about the transformation. The reader seems no longer to be in a romance, which tries to keep some sense of plausibility so that he can believe in the reality of the idealized fiction, but in a fairy tale, where he knows it cannot be true. To undercut further any tendency to believe that the ending could be "real," Gautier added comic touches to keep us from taking it seriously. The statue of Pomona in the garden proudly sports a new nose, and as a final preposterous touch, the cat dies from overeating, and when it is buried, the long lost treasure of the Sigognac family is discovered in a chest as they dig. The ending may be a happy one, but its very exaggeration pointedly reminds us that such outcomes do not occur in real life. Thus Gautier managed to satisfy the demand for a happy ending and still maintain his original idea that happiness in life can only be illusory.

The final lesson emerges: *Le Capitaine Fracasse* is a literary illusion which creates an exciting "real" story that convinces us as we read, but which then provides us with a blatantly illusory ending, which is a real necessity for its readers. In this tissue of paradox and ambiguity one may despair of ever finding "true" human reality. Gautier seems to be throwing up his hands before the impossibility of arriving at any certainty, and while he wishes it were otherwise — there is a wistfulness to his artificially happy ending — he despairs at ever discovering the full meaning of existence. Gautier's "traditional" nineteenth-century romance is, curiously, a pessimistic last will and testament bequeathed to the uncertainties and ambiguities of the twentieth century.

CHAPTER 9

Conclusion

OVER the years Théophile Gautier's literary reputation has suffered from two serious misconceptions, both traceable to his championing of the doctrine of Art for Art's sake. The first is that the author of *Emaux et camées* was, in André Gide's phrase, "blind to everything but the exterior world,"[1] and created poetry that described only the surface of man's being. The rich inner world of the poet, such critics claim, is totally missing from Gautier's work, with the result that he presents a very dehumanized view of man. Gautier was himself well aware of this charge of impersonality, and he responded to it in the pages of "Spirite." The heroine of the story comments on the work of Guy de Malivert, Gautier's alter ego:

It is easier to know a subjective author than an objective one: the first expresses his feelings, exposes his ideas and judges society and creation against an ideal scale; the second presents objects just as nature offers them; he proceeds by images, by descriptions; he presents things to the reader's view; he draws, dresses and colors his characters with precision, he puts in their mouths what they must have said and keeps his own opinion to himself. That latter technique was your way of writing. At first sight one might accuse you of a certain disdainful impartiality which makes little difference between a lizard and a man, between the red glow of a sunset and a city on fire; but if one looks more closely, one can make out rapid bursts of inner sensitivity which disappear as soon as they erupt, for they are contained and controlled by a proud modesty that does not like to show its emotions.[2]

As Gautier claims, it is indeed possible to discern psychological constants that reveal his character through the supposed impersonality of his art, although these truths are revealed more through the constant use of image patterns than by sudden bursts of confession on the author's part. As we have seen, both in his prose and in his poetry he tends to isolate his protagonists from the crowds and have them find a sanctuary of some kind within a secret enclosed space. This withdrawal is seen at one level (one thinks of Fortunio) as the highest possible expression of bliss or gratification of the senses. It is obvious, of course, that these places of ultimate felicity have in Gautier's imaginative world a strong erotic content, which is exposed through the imagery of the bedroom or of a lush tropical garden. But it is a psychological truism that these sanctuaries of erotic felicity are ambivalent in nature, for if they promise sexual gratification, they also isolate one from life and therefore constitute a kind of tomb. The poem, "Coerulei oculi," and the story, "Une Nuit de Cléopâtre," are the clearest expressions of this theme of *eros-thanatos.* The oedipal nature of these and other narrative structures can reasonably be considered to point to Gautier's own unresolved psychological problems, and so in the last analysis we do indeed find a human being behind the works, and a very sensitive one indeed.

The other popular misconception is that Gautier, like other nineteenth-century artists who proclaimed the doctrine of Art for Art's sake, had nothing to say to his century about social struggle and change. Albert Camus in his Nobel Prize acceptance speech of 1957 called nineteenth-century bourgeois society "phony" ("factice") and Art for Art's sake its equally inauthentic expression. Other hostile critics have noted that Gautier was perfectly willing to serve any political regime provided it did not interfere with the agreeable rhythm of his life. This view is overly harsh. While it is true that the poet lacked the heroism of a Hugo who went into exile rather than live under Napoleon III's dictatorship, Gautier was no easy admirer of middle-class "progress." It was, in fact, the dominant bourgeois class that particularly repelled him, and he detested the ugliness that the budding Industrial Revolution was bringing to France. In a sense Gautier reacted to his times like a horrified aristocrat, except that his nobility was based on esthetics rather than on a family genealogy. It can be argued, of course, that unlike Balzac, Gautier failed to appreciate the esthetic possibilities latent in the energy of commerce and finance, but it is certain that Gautier was not aloof from his time out of total indifference. The desire to flee one's culture for a better one is a clear condemnation of that culture.

But neither biographical nor social relevance prove anything concerning the value of Gautier's work as art. Northrop Frye observed wittily that to understand American culture one issue of the *Ladies' Home Journal* might be worth all of Henry James,[3] and yet from an artistic point of view James is clearly worth more than the popular magazine. Beauty in a work of art is impossible of mathematical demonstration, but sophisticated readers can recognize it. In 1873 when Gautier died, more than eighty of his fellow poets expressed their appreciation of "le bon Théo's" contribution by writing poems in his honor. The volume, *Le Tombeau de Théophile Gautier* ("Epitaph for Théophile Gautier"), was published by Alphonse Lemerre. These poets, who included such giants as Hugo, Leconte de Lisle, Mallarmé, and Swinburne, understood that Gautier's passionate commitment to Beauty and to perfection of form was worthy of their hommage. While Gautier in practice often fell below his own high standards of excellence, and there can be no doubt that some of his work is second-rate, in his very best works he achieved that perfect fusion of form and content that is the goal of all art. Nor were his best efforts limited in scope or form. It would be hard to improve on "Celle-ci et celle-là" and *Albertus* as lighthearted satire; the little play, *Pierrot posthume*, is a perfect gem of joyous humor. The theme of love and death finds exquisite expression of a lyrical kind in the libretto of the ballet, *Giselle*. It assumes a more somber Baudelairean tone in "Coerulei oculi" and "L'Impassible" and a crushing, fatalistic one in Oriental tales like "Le Roi Candaule." The longing for a purified ideal achieves exquisite expression in "Spirite," and yet Gautier, supposedly so simple in his view of man, can also play brilliantly with paradox and the ambiguity of man's experiences in such diverse works as "La Morte amoureuse" and *Le Capitaine Fracasse*. In all of his finest achievements, it must be remembered, it is not the ideas in themselves but rather the fusion of idea and form that has enabled the works to survive the test of time. Their sense of total harmony gives us that feeling of completeness that comes when we encounter true beauty, and it is for these frequent miracles of art that Gautier will long be remembered.

Notes and References

The editions given in the notes below are those used for this study and not necessarily the first edition. For date of first publication of Gautier's major works, see Chronology.

Chapter One

1. First published in *L'Illustration* on March 9, 1867. Reprinted at the beginning of *Portraits contemporains* (Paris: Charpentier, 1881).
2. Henri Van der Tuin, *L'Evolution psychologique, esthétique et littéraire de Théophile Gautier: étude de caractérologie littéraire* (Paris: Nizet, 1933), Ch. I.
3. *Portraits contemporains*, p. 3.
4. Ibid.
5. Ibid., pp. 3 - 4.
6. Ibid., p. 4.
7. René Jasinski, *Les Années romantiques de Théophile Gautier* (Paris: Vuibert, 1929), p. 23.
8. *Portraits contemporains*, p. 5.
9. *Histoire du romantisme* (Paris: Librairie des bibliophiles, Flammarion, 1929), p. 2.
10. Ibid.
11. Ibid., p. 4.
12. It constitutes one chapter of *Histoire du romantisme*. Ref., p. 6.
13. Ibid., p. 1.
14. Ibid., p. 17.
15. Ibid., p. 20.
16. Maxime Du Camp, *Théophile Gautier* (Paris: Hachette, 1890), p. 36.
17. Cited by Jasinski, *Années romantiques*, p. 71.
18. For all of Gautier's poetry, we refer to the edition by René Jasinski of the *Poésies complètes* (Paris: Nizet, 1970), 3 vols.
19. Jasinski, *Années romantiques*, p. 134.
20. *Les Jeunes-France: romans goguenards* (Paris: Charpentier, 1883), p. 81.
21. Jasinski, *Années romantiques*, p. 267.

22. *Histoire de l'art dramatique en France depuis vingt-cinq ans* (Paris: Hetzel, 1859), III, 106 - 107. Cited by Jasinski, *Années romantiques*, p. 282.
23. *Théophile Gautier: His Life and Times* (New York: Coward-McCann, 1959), pp. 24 - 31.

Chapter Two

1. Paris: Calmann-Lévy, 1881, I, 66 - 67.
2. Victor Hugo, *Cromwell.* Edition de l'Imprimerie nationale (Paris: Ollendorff, 1912), p. 11.
3. See Maurice Z. Shroder, *Icarus: The Image of the Artist in French Romanticism* (Cambridge, Mass.: Harvard University Press, 1961).
4. *Les Jeunes-France*, ed. cit., p. 190.
5. *Caprices et zigzags* (Paris: Charpentier, 1884), pp. 1 - 2.
6. Published in late 1835, although Vol. II bears the date 1836. All references are to *Mademoiselle de Maupin*, ed. A. Boschot (Paris: Garnier, 1955).
7. For the genesis of *Mademoiselle de Maupin*, see René Jasinski, *Années romantiques*, Ch. IX.
8. Ibid, pp. 290 - 300.
9. Albert B. Smith, "Gautier's *Mademoiselle de Maupin:* The Quest for Happiness," *Modern Language Quarterly*, 32, No. 2 (June, 1971), 168.
10. Boschot, ed. cit., p. xxiv.
11. *Trois essais de mythologie romantique* (Paris: Corti, 1966), p. 94.
12. Albert Smith, art. cit., 169.
13. See Raymond Giraud, "Winckelmann's Part in Gautier's Perception of Classical Beauty," *Yale French Studies*, No. 38 (May, 1967), 172 - 182.
14. "Le mythe de l'androgyne dans *Mademoiselle de Maupin*," *Revue d'histoire littéraire de la France*, 4, No. 72 (Juillet-août, 1972), 600 - 608.
15. Ibid., 608.
16. Art. cit., 173 - 174.

Chapter Three

1. "Théophile Gautier," in *Oeuvres complètes de Baudelaire* (Paris: Gallimard, 1961), p. 679.
2. *The Creative Imagination of Théophile Gautier: A Study in Literary Psychology* (Princeton, N.J.: Princeton University Press, 1927), p. 10.
3. See *The Mirror and the Lamp: Romantic Theory and the Critical Tradition* (New York: Norton, 1953).
4. Michael Clifford Spencer, *The Art Criticism of Théophile Gautier* (Genève: Droz, 1969).
5. *La Presse*, April 4.
6. *Revue de Paris*, 3ième série (April, 1841), pp. 159 - 160. Cited by Spencer, p. 17.
7. Baudelaire, ed. cit., pp. 913 - 14.

8. Ibid., p. 877.
9. *Portraits contemporains*, p. 12.
10. Introduction to *Mademoiselle de Maupin*, ed. A. Boschot (Paris: Garnier, 1955), p. xxiv.
11. *Portraits contemporains*, p. 287.
12. *Loin de Paris* (Paris: Charpentier, 1881), p. 231.
13. From "Du Beau dans l'art," a review of Töpffer's *Réflexions et menus propos d'un peintre genevois*. Cited in Gautier's *L'Art moderne* (Paris: Michel Lévy, 1856), pp. 151 - 53.
14. Ibid., p. 151.
15. For the general history of this doctrine at that time, see Albert Cassagne, *La Théorie de l'Art pour l'Art en France chez les derniers romantiques et les premiers réalistes* (Paris: Hachette, 1906).
16. Cited by Louise Dillingham, op. cit., p. 38.
17. *La Préface de Mademoiselle de Maupin*, éd. crit. par Georges Matoré (Paris: Droz, 1946), p. 32.
18. Cited by Spencer, p. 61.
19. Spencer, p. 102.
20. Although this six-volume work is not complete, it serves the needs of all but the most specialized critics.
21. *Histoire de l'art dramatique en France depuis vingt-cinq ans*, VI, 267. Review of November 10, 1867. The other quotations in this chapter from Gautier's theater criticism are also from *La Presse* and can be found in these published volumes.
22. *Mademoiselle de Maupin*, Ch. XI.
23. *Histoire de l'art dramatique*, I, 21.
24. *Les Grotesques* was first published in 1844. Except for the article on Villon, the essays were written in 1834 and 1835.
25. Middle-class incomprehension showed itself in the form of a lawsuit by the government against *La France littéraire*, which had published the essay.
26. *Portraits contemporains*, p. 326.
27. Ibid., p. 330.
28. Ibid., pp. 75 - 76.
29. *Portraits et souvenirs littéraires* (Paris: Charpentier, 1885), p. 51.
30. Originally published under the title "Rapport sur le progrès des lettres depuis vingt-cinq ans." Included in *Histoire du romantisme*, ed. cit., pp. 255 - 345.

Chapter Four

1. E.g., Georges Poulet, *Etudes sur le temps humain* (Paris: Plon, 1950), p. 278.
2. From "La Pente de la rêverie" ("The Descent of Dream"), 1831.
3. For the impact of Spanish culture on France at the beginning of the nineteenth century, see Ilse H. Lipschutz, *Spanish Painting and the French*

Romantics (Cambridge, Mass.: Harvard University Press, 1972).

4. I am indebted to Ms. Jacqueline Rube of Austin, Texas, for the initial idea of treating *Voyage en Espagne* as a quest narrative. For a study of Gautier's sources, see Gilberte Guillaumie-Reicher, *Théophile Gautier et l'Espagne* (Paris: Hachette, 1935).

5. First published in 1949. Citations taken from Meridian Books edition, New York, 1956.

6. *L'España de Th. Gautier,* éd. critique (Paris: Vuibert, 1929), p. 38.

7. All references in this chapter are to *Voyage en Espagne* (Paris: Charpentier, 1904).

8. 8. But on the humble dial which I had by chance looked at,
Like the words of fire on Belshazzar's walls,
Like the inscription over an accursed portal
A sentence is written in black letters.
Four solemn words, four words of Latin,
In which each passer-by may read his destiny:
"Each hour wounds and the last one kills."

9. Later, when writing "La Fontaine du cimetière" ("The Spring in the Cemetery") for *España,* he confessed that he had felt a shiver of horror at drinking this pure water "which tasted like death." Perhaps by then he had realized that the cemetery offered death rather than repose.

10. You find in the mountains occasional small pools,
Pure as crystal, blue as turquoise,
Jewels fallen from the finger of the Angel Ithuriel,
Where the fearful chamois when he comes to drink
Imagines — deceived by the optical illusion —
That he is drinking the azure of the sky.
These limpid pools, when daylight is reflected in them,
Have, like one's pupil, moist flecks of gold,
And it is with these blue eyes and their calm, gentle gaze,
That the mountain contemplates in ecstasy
As He forges a sun in the recesses of His temple,
God, the jealous workman.

11. Ernest Feydeau, *Théophile Gautier, souvenirs intimes* (Paris: Plon, 1874), p. 143.

12. *Les Beautés de l'opéra, le Diable Boîteux* (Paris: Hetzel, 1845), p. 25.

13. See Luzius Keller, *Piranèse et les Romantiques français, le mythe des escaliers en spirale* (Paris: Corti, 1966).

14. [The rose laurel] blushes in the blue water like a girl;
Its flowers, which seem alive, are flesh-colored.
One imagines, as one looks at the sparkling water,
[That one can see] a naked odalisk waiting to be dressed,
With weeping hair beside a pool of clear water.

This rose laurel, I loved it with unequaled love.
Each evening, I went to rest nearby.
To one of its blooms, a moist and crimson mouth,
I put my lips, and sometimes — what a miracle —
I thought I felt the flower return my kiss.

15. For details, see Jasinski, *L'España de Th. Gautier*, pp. 13 - 14.
16. *Studies in Classic American Literature* (1923); reprinted (New York: Viking, 1964), p. 2.
17. Jasinski, *L'España de Th. Gautier*, p. 30.
18. Claude Book-Senninger, *Théophile Gautier, auteur dramatique*, (Paris: Nizet, 1972), p. 145, correctly stresses this point.

Chapter Five

1. Claude Book-Senninger, *Théophile Gautier, auteur dramatique*, p. 339, comes to the conclusion that Gautier probably was the author, but that one cannot be certain.
2. References to Gautier's plays in this chapter are taken from his *Théâtre* (Paris: Charpentier, 1882).
3. Book-Senninger, p. 53.
4. Ibid., p. 56.
5. *Le Figaro*, Oct. 30, 1836; cited by Book-Senninger, p. 218.
6. *La Presse*, July 1, 1844.
7. *La Presse*, July 20, 1846.
8. See Edwin Binney, *Les Ballets de Théophile Gautier* (Paris: Nizet, 1965), for details.
9. Binney, p. 33.
10. *Histoire de l'art dramatique en France depuis vingt-cinq ans*, ed. cit., II, 103.
11. *Théâtre*, p. 269. See also *Histoire de l'art dramatique*, II, 103.
12. Binney, p. 61.
13. Serge Lifar, *Giselle, Apothéose du ballet romantique* (Paris: Albin Michel, 1942); cited by Binney, p. 334.
14. For the best study of the decadent aspects of Romanticism, see Mario Praz, *The Romantic Agony* (New York: Meridian Books, 1956).

Chapter Six

1. From a review of Hawthorne's *Twice-Told Tales*, cited in the *Portable Edgar Allan Poe* (New York: Viking, 1945), p. 62.
2. "On Prose Theory," trans. into French (and by us into English) by Tzvetan Todorov in *Théorie de la littérature* (Paris: Editions du seuil, 1965), pp. 197 - 211.
3. See Albert George, *Short Fiction in France, 1800 - 1850* (Syracuse, N.Y.: Syracuse University Press, 1964), Ch. I, for details of the history of short fiction in France.
4. First published under the title "El Dorado." For this and for all other stories discussed in this chapter, the date given is that of first publication and not the date the story first appeared in volume form unless it was for the first time.
5. E.g., George, p. 179.

6. Included, along with "Une Nuit de Cléopâtre," in the volume *Le Roman de la momie* (Paris: Garnier, 1963). All references are to this edition.

7. See note 6, above. "Le Roman de la momie" first appeared in *Le Moniteur* in 1857. Hence the apparent discrepancy with the date indicated in our Chronology.

8. For the positive aspects of Gautier's use of solar imagery, see Marc Eigeldinger, "L'Image solaire dans la poésie de Théophile Gautier," *Revue d'histoire littéraire de la France*, 72, No. 4 (Juillet-août, 1972), 626 - 40.

9. See note 6 above.

10. Published in 1856.

11. Most of Gautier's fantastic tales have been recently reissued under the title *Contes fantastiques* (Paris: Corti, 1972). Unless otherwise indicated, all further references in this chapter are to this edition.

12. "Essai sur le fantastique," *Revue de Paris* (Octobre, 1965), p. 104.

13. H. P. Lovecraft, *Supernatural Horror in Literature* (New York: Abramson, 1945), Ch. 1.

14. *Magazine littéraire*, No. 66 (Juillet-août, 1972), 9 - 16.

15. Roger Caillois uses the term "pseudo-fantastique" for this kind of illusion. See the preface to *Anthologie du fantastique* (Paris: Gallimard, 1958), p.5.

16. *Introduction à la littérature fantastique* (Paris: Editions du seuil, 1970), pp. 46 - 49.

17. Paris: Gallimard, 1965, p. 161.

18. See Claude Roy, "Psychologie du fantastique," in *Les Temps modernes*, No. 167 - 68 (Février-mars, 1960), 1393 - 416.

19. First published in 1856 under the title *Paul d'Aspremont*.

20. Spoelberch de Lovenjoul, *Histoire des oeuvres de Théophile Gautier* (Paris: Charpentier, 1887), I, 11 - 15.

21. *Introduction à la littérature fantastique*, p. 144.

22. Marcel Schneider, *La Littérature fantastique en France* (Paris: Fayard, 1964) stresses Gautier's anguish over the problem of the split personality visible through the doubling of the characters (p. 217).

23. *Spirite, nouvelle fantastique*, éd. Marc Eigeldinger (Paris: Nizet, 1970), p. 8. All references are to this edition.

24. Albert B. Smith, *Ideal and Reality in the Fictional Narratives of Théophile Gautier* (Gainesville, Fla.: University of Florida Press, 1969).

25. Eigeldinger, ed. cit., p. 13.

26. Théophile Gautier, *Entretiens, souvenirs et correspondance* (Paris: Charpentier, 1911), p. 169.

27. Chapel Hill, N.C.: University of North Carolina Press, 1969.

28. Ibid., p. 114.

Chapter Seven

1. *Histoire du romantisme*, p. 322.

2. During the wars of the Empire, Goethe, at the sound of the brutal

cannon,/Wrote *Occidental-Oriental Poems**/A cool oasis where art can breathe./Leaving Shakespeare for Nisami/He perfumed himself with essence of sandalwood,/And in an Eastern meter/Jotted down the song which Hudhud sighs./As Goethe on his couch/Withdrew from everything/And plucked Hafiz's roses,/Without worrying about the hurricane/Which beat against my closed windows,/*I* wrote *Enamels and Cameos.*

*Gautier's translation of *Westöstliche Divan* as *Le Divan occidental* is inaccurate and destroys the sense of the poem, so that we have taken the liberty of giving a more exact translation.

3. Yes, the work of art emerges more beautiful/From a form that resists [the poet's] labor,/Poetry, marble, onyx, enamel./Everything passes. . . . Robust art/Alone is forever./The bust survives civilization./Sculpt, file, chisel./May your floating dream/Be imbedded/In the resisting stone.

4. Joanna Richardson, op. cit., p. 114.

5. Ed. cit., I, lxxxiii.

6. "La Symphonie en blanc majeur: An Interpretation," *L'Esprit créateur,* 3, No. 1 (Spring, 1963), 28.

7. Jasinski's title is slightly misleading. Some poems of this group antedate 1852.

8. The poem was inspired by Madame Moulton, who later became the wife of the Minister of Denmark in Paris. It was written in July, 1866, and published in *Le Diable* on March 26, 1870.

The Unfeeling One

Satiety sleeps in the depths of your large eyes,
In them there are no more desires, no more love, no more longing.
They have drunk the light and dried up the springs of life,
Like a deep sea into which the skies are absorbed.

Under their somber blue one can read the vast boredom of the Gods,
For whom every desire is satisfied in advance,
And who, knowing the effect before the cause appears,
Blend into their present the future already past.

Infinity has melted into your large pupils,
And before this mirror which reflects nothing,
Love, discouraged, sits down, folding its wings.

You, however, with that Olympian calm,
Like Mnemosyne leaning on her pedestal,
You languidly pursue an impossible dream.

Chapter Eight

1. Cited by Adolphe Boschot in his edition of *Le Capitaine Fracasse* (Paris: Garnier, 1961), vii. All page references are to this edition.

2. Ibid., viii.

3. Ibid., xv.

4. Judith Gautier, letter to the *Gil Blas,* December 10, 1884.

5. *Anatomy of Criticism: Four Essays* (Princeton, N.J.: Princeton University Press, 1957), p. 305.

6. Joseph Campbell, *The Hero with a Thousand Faces*, pp. 49 - 58.

7. For details, see Spoelberch de Lovenjoul, *Histoire des oeuvres de Théophile Gautier*, II, 256 - 257.

Chapter Nine

1. *Incidences* (Paris: Gallimard, 1951), p. 163.
2. *Spirite*, ed. cit., p. 118.
3. *Anatomy of Criticism*, p. 19.

Selected Bibliography

PRIMARY SOURCES

To make a bibliographical listing of Gautier's work that is clear, concise, and reasonably complete is impossible. During his lifetime, Gautier not only wrote an immense amount, he frequently published a work first in some newspaper, then in book form, and — in the case of short stories and critical articles — then sometimes in different collections of stories or criticism published by different editors. To appreciate the complexity of the problem, one has only to consult Spoelberch de Lovenjoul's massive *Histoire des oeuvres de Théophile Gautier* published by Charpentier in Paris in 1887 (2 vols.). It is still an indispensable tool for scholars. In an effort to simplify this whole matter, we have included in our Chronology the date of first publication in book form of Gautier's main works prior to his death. For more detail and for the numerous editions that appeared up to 1937, see Hector Talvart and Joseph Place's *Bibliographie des auteurs modernes de langue française* (Paris: Chronique des lettres françaises, 1937), 6, 312 - 66.

Beginninig in 1863 and continuing until 1889, the publisher Georges Charpentier made an effort to bring out Gautier's complete works, but these volumes are long since out of print, and in fact they were far from complete. Vitally needed today is a comprehensive critical edition of Gautier's work, including his correspondence, but in recent years some of Gautier's individual works have been republished in good editions, and the modern reader is grateful for them. We give below the best of them, especially those still in print or widely available as of this writing:

For poetry:

Poésies complètes, ed. René Jasinski. Paris: Nizet, 1970. 3 vols. This edition is quite complete, except for Gautier's erotic verse and has information concerning composition and sources.

L'España de Th. Gautier, ed. René Jasinski. Paris: Vuibert, 1929. Compares the poems with the prose text of *Voyage en Espagne*. Also has photographs of places Gautier described in Spain.

Emaux et camées, intro. de Jean Pommier, notes et lexique de Georges Matoré. Lille: Giard, 1947. Solid critical edition.

Emaux et camées, ed. Madeleine Cottin. Paris: Lettres modernes, 1968. Attractive and useful edition, except that she does not place the key poem "L'Art" at the end, where Gautier intended it.

For English translations of some of Gautier's poetry see:
The Gentle Enchanter; Thirty-four Poems, translated with introduction by Brian Hill. London: Rupert Hart-Davis, 1960.

For Prose Fiction:
Le Capitaine Fracasse, ed. Adolphe Boschot. Paris: Garnier, 1961. An informed introduction, but the critical apparatus is minimal.
Contes fantastiques. Paris: Corti, 1972. No critical apparatus.
Mademoiselle de Maupin. There have been many editions of this famous work, and there are still many in print today, but the standard one is edited by Adolphe Boschot. Paris: Garnier, 1966. An informed introduction, but the critical apparatus is minimal.
Le Roman de la momie (Includes also "Une Nuit de Cléopâtre," "Le Roi Candaule," and "Arria Marcella"), ed. Adolphe Boschot. Paris: Garnier, 1963. A very good edition.
Spirite, ed. Marc Eigeldinger. Paris: Nizet, 1970. A good introduction gives pertinent details concerning the story's genesis and shows that Gautier meant the work as a tribute from himself to Carlotta Grisi.

For English translations of Gautier's prose fiction:
Gautier's short stories were translated and published in a ten-volume edition by Little, Brown of Boston in 1903 under the title *The Romances of Théophile Gautier*. They have recently been reprinted as *Short Stories*, tr. by George Burnham Ives with notes by Frédéric-César de Sumichrast. Freeport, N.Y.: Books for Libraries Press, 1970.
Mademoiselle de Maupin, tr. by R. and E. Powys Mathers. London: Cassell, 1948. Another translation is by Paul Seiver. New York: Pantheon Books, 1949.

For Gautier's criticism:
Except for the preface to *Mademoiselle de Maupin*, which can be found in any edition of *Maupin* itself, Gautier's critical writings are not available in English, and even modern French editions are lacking. However, we can mention:
Les Grotesques, a modern reprint of the 1897 Charpentier edition. Geneva: Slatkine, 1969.
Histoire de l'art dramatique en France depuis vingt-cinq ans, reprinted from the 1858 - 59 edition (Paris: Hetzel). Geneva: Slatkine, 1968, 6 vols.
La Préface de Mademoiselle de Maupin, ed. crit. par Georges Matoré. Paris: Droz, 1946. Gives the development and the sources of this important essay. A valuable supplement to Jasinski's treatment of the same

material in his *Années romantiques de Théophile Gautier* (see below).

Travel Literature in translation:

Romantic in Spain (Voyage in Espagne), tr. Catherine A. Phillips. New York: Knopf, 1926.

Russia by Théophile Gautier and by other distinguished French travelers of note, tr. by Florence MacIntyre. New York: Arno, 1970. Includes some of the *Voyage en Russie.*

Correspondence:

Much of the correspondence is still in the Collection Lovenjoul in the Chantilly Museum. However, we can cite:

Les Plus Belles Lettres de Théophile Gautier, présentées par Pierre Descaves. Paris: Calmann-Lévy, 1962. A selection of Gautier's letters. Unfortunately, many are—despite the title—routine notes. Others have been expurgated.

Ballets in translation:

Giselle, or the Wilis, tr. and adapted from Théophile Gautier by Violette Verdy. New York: McGraw-Hill, 1970.

SECONDARY SOURCES

There has been enough written on Gautier to make a complete bibliography of secondary studies much too lengthy. We give below only works cited in this book which deal, in part or in whole, with Gautier.

ALBOUY, PIERRE. "Le mythe de l'androgyne dans *Mademoiselle de Maupin,*" *Revue d'histoire littéraire de la France,* LXXII, 4 (Juillet-août 1972), 600 - 608.

BERGERAT, EMILE. *Théophile Gautier, entretiens, souvenirs et correspondance.* Paris: Charpentier, 1911. Charming recollections of his conversations with Gautier, especially during the poet's later years.

BINNEY, EDWIN. *The Ballets of Théophile Gautier.* Paris: Nizet, 1965. The definitive study of the sources and the circumstances of composition of all of Gautier's ballet librettos.

BOOK-SENNINGER, CLAUDE. *Théophile Gautier, auteur dramatique.* Paris: Nizet, 1972. Indispensable for anyone interested in Gautier's theater.

BOSCHOT, ADOLPHE. *Théophile Gautier.* Paris: Desclée de Brouwer, 1933. A standard biography.

DELVAILLE, BERNARD. *Théophile Gautier.* Paris: Seghers, 1968. An agreeable introduction to Gautier and his work. Gives a chronology, a brief biography, some critical judgments and a good choice of texts.

DILLINGHAM, LOUISE. *The Creative Imagination of Théophile Gautier: A Study in Literary Psychology.* Princeton, N.J.: Princeton University Press, 1927. An attempt to explain Gautier's art by his psychology. Although somewhat dated (there is, for instance, no mention of Freud), there are many valuable observations.

DU CAMP, MAXIME. *Théophile Gautier.* Paris: Hachette, 1890. Also available in a recent English translation by J. E. Gordon. Freeport, N.Y.: Books for Libraries Press, 1971. An urbane and intelligent general book on Gautier by a friend and fellow writer.

EIGELDINGER, MARC. "L'Image solaire dans la poésie de Théophile Gautier," *Revue d'histoire littéraire de la France,* LXII, 4 (Juillet-août, 1972) 626 - 40. Stresses the importance of warm, sunny climates to Gautier. This article and the one by Albouy are only two of many in this fine issue dedicated to Gautier's work.

FEYDEAU, ERNEST. *Théophile Gautier, souvenirs intimes.* Paris: Plon, 1874. Like Bergerat's book, a pleasant anecdotal account of Gautier by a friend.

GAUTIER, JUDITH. *Le Collier des jours, le second rang du collier. Souvenirs littéraires.* Paris: Juven, 1909. Recollections of Gautier by his daughter. Valuable.

GEORGE, ALBERT. *Short Fiction in France, 1800 - 1850.* Syracuse, N.Y.: Syracuse University Press, 1964. Part of one chapter is devoted to Gautier. A standard work.

GIRAUD, RAYMOND. "Winckelmann's Part in Gautier's Perception of Classical Beauty," *Yale French Studies,* XXXVIII (May 1967), 172 - 82. An interesting article on one aspect of Gautier's intellectual development.

GUILLAUMIE-REICHER, GILBERTE. *Théophile Gautier et l'Espagne.* Paris: Hachette, 1935. Gives many of the bookish sources of Gautier's trip to Spain and also reproduces his *carnet de voyage* (travel notebook).

JASINSKI, RENÉ. *Les Années romantiques de Théophile Gautier.* Paris: Vuibert, 1929. A superb job of literary history. Indispensable for anything concerning Gautier's life and work up to the year 1836.

KELLER, LUZIUS. *Piranèse et les Romantiques français, le mythe des escaliers en spirale.* Paris: Corti, 1966. Has a special section on Gautier.

LIPSCHUTZ, ILSE H. *Spanish Painting and the French Romantics.* Cambridge, Mass.: Harvard University Press, 1972. Excellent for an understanding of the historical background of Gautier's trip to Spain. Includes plates of paintings Gautier discusses in *Voyage en Espagne.*

MICKEL, EMANUEL. *The Artificial Paradises in French Literature.* Chapel Hill, N.C.: University of North Carolina Press, 1969. Contains twenty useful pages on Gautier.

POULET, GEORGES. *Etudes sur le temps humain.* Paris: Plon, 1950. Chapter XIV deals with Gautier. Stresses his fear of death and the passage of time.

———. *Trois essais de mythologie romantique.* Paris: Corti, 1966. One of the three essays deals in large measure with Gautier and some of his favorite images.

RICHARDSON, JOANNA. *Théophile Gautier, His Life and Times.* New York: Coward-McCann, 1959. The standard biography of Gautier in English.

A more comprehensive one is needed, however.

SCHNEIDER, MARCEL. *La Littérature fantastique en France*. Paris: Fayard, 1964. A standard work on the subject, with a few pages (211 - 21) of high quality on Gautier.

SMITH, ALBERT B. *Ideal and Reality in the Fictional Narratives of Théophile Gautier*. Gainesville, Fla.: University of Florida Press, 1969. An attempt, perhaps a little overstated, to prove an evolution in Gautier's thought from a materialistic to an idealistic position.

———. "Gautier's Mademoiselle de Maupin: The Quest for Happiness," *Modern Language Quarterly*, XXXII, 2 (June, 1971), 168 - 74. An important article seeking to establish the idea of the heroine as more than an allegorical figure.

SPENCER, MICHAEL CLIFFORD. *The Art Criticism of Théophile Gautier*. Geneva: Droz, 1969. Brief but valuable study of the esthetic principles behind Gautier's art criticism. Weak on Gautier's criticism of Spanish painting.

TILD, JEAN. *Théophile Gautier et ses amis*. Paris: Albin Michel, 1951. An agreeable biography.

TODOROV, TZVETAN. *Introduction à la littérature fantastique*. Paris: Editions du seuil, 1970. Many references throughout to Gautier's fantastic tales. Modern and intelligent criticism.

VAN EERDE, JOHN. "La Symphonie en blanc majeur: An Interpretation," *L'Esprit créateur*, III, 1 (Spring 1963), 26 - 33. Brings out well Gautier's dualistic tendencies. Stresses the importance of certain colors. This entire issue is devoted to Gautier and contains other valuable articles.

VAN DER TUIN, HENRI. *L'Evolution psychologique, esthétique et littéraire de Théophile Gautier: étude de caractérologie littéraire*. Paris: Nizet, 1933. Like Dillingham's work, an attempt to understand the artist in psychological terms. More modern in that he uses some Freudian psychology.

Index

(The works of Gautier are listed under his name)

DATE DUE
